GETTING STARTED IN

CONSULTING

Other Books by Alan Weiss

GETTING STARTED IN
CONSULTING

ALAN WEISS

WILEY

Published by John Wiley & Sons, Inc., Hoboken, New Jersey.

Published simultaneously in Canada.

For general information on our other products and services or for technical support, please contact our Customer Care Department within the United States at (800) 762-2974, outside the United States at (317) 572-3993 or fax (317) 572-4002.

Wiley publishes in a variety of print and electronic formats and by print-on-demand. Some material included with standard print versions of this book may not be included in e-books or in print-on-demand. If this book refers to media such as a CD or DVD that is not included in the version you purchased, you may download this material at http://booksupport.wiley.com. For more information about Wiley products, visit www.wiley.com.

Library of Congress Cataloging-in-Publication Data:

Names: Weiss, Alan, 1946- author.
Title: Getting started in consulting / Alan Weiss.
Description: Fourth edition. | Hoboken, New Jersey : Wiley, [2019] | Includes
   index. |
Identifiers: LCCN 2018051259 (print) | LCCN 2018053848 (ebook) | ISBN
   9781119542131 (Adobe PDF) | ISBN 9781119542148 (ePub) | ISBN 9781119542155
   (hardcover)
Subjects: LCSH: Business consultants—Handbooks, manuals, etc. |
   Consultants—Marketing—Handbooks, manuals, etc.
Classification: LCC HD69.C6 (ebook) | LCC HD69.C6 W459 2019 (print) | DDC
   001—dc23
LC record available at https://lccn.loc.gov/2018051259

Printed in the United States of America

V10008239_021319

Our 50th wedding anniversary occurred during the writing of this book. This book, all my others, my career, my family, and my happiness would not be remotely possible without Maria. Merely thanking her here for my wondrous life is woefully insufficient, but I am informing all of you that it is almost impossible to get started in any pursuit without unwavering support.

And so: To Maria, with all my love.

Contents

Introduction to the Fourth Edition

I wrote the original version of this book in 2000; the prior edition (the third) was written almost 10 years ago. In these ensuing years we've seen 3-D printing, the retirement of the 747 jumbo jet, Donald Trump elected president against all predictions, Global Entry speeding the immigration process, strategies formerly taking six months to formulate and covering five years obsolete, the iPhone X, Tesla, kale as a routine food offering, the admonition that health-care workers must wash their hands to prevent the spread of illness, a huge recession and an unprecedented economic recovery, and the New England Patriots playing in three more Super Bowls and winning two of them.

Consulting remains a very hot profession because huge organizations continue to reduce residual talent in favor of mission-critical specialists and automation, and small businesses are seeking more help than ever (and they are the largest producers of net new jobs in most of the world, since large companies tend only to reduce or replace the workforce). There is little barrier to entry in solo consulting,[1] which is both a blessing and a curse.

The intent herein is to enable you to hit the ground running under contemporary conditions. I'll assume you're either brand new to the profession or in the early stages of your launch, though the lessons included constitute a strong review for even veteran consultants. You can look up certain aspects of the business (for example, office logistics or finding buyers), or you can read it sequentially. See Appendix F for free resources located on my site and my blog.

I've found the consulting profession to be exciting, challenging, highly rewarding, and amenable to all types of people, passions, and predispositions. I've been able to form a huge global community of such entrepreneurial people over the years. It's my pleasure to welcome you to it here.

Full speed ahead. It's become that kind of world, and it's no place for the tentative. We're not here to stick our toes in the water, we're here to make waves.

Alan Weiss
East Greenwich, RI
November 2018

Note

1. Throughout the book I include boutique firm ownership under solo consulting.

About the Author

Alan Weiss is one of those rare people who can say he is a consultant, speaker, and author and mean it. His consulting firm, Summit Consulting Group, Inc., has attracted clients such as Merck, Hewlett-Packard, GE, Mercedes-Benz, State Street Corporation, the Times Mirror Company, the Federal Reserve, the New York Times Company, and over 200 other leading organizations.

He has served on the boards of directors of the Trinity Repertory Company, a Tony Award–winning New England regional theater, the Newport International Film Festival (where he was chairman), Festival Ballet Providence, and the Harvard Center for Mental Health and the Media.

His speaking typically includes 20 keynotes a year at major conferences, and he has been a visiting faculty member at Case Western Reserve University, Boston College, Tufts, St. John's University, the University of Illinois, the Institute of Management Studies, and the University of Georgia's Terry College of Business. He has held an appointment as adjunct professor in the College of Business at the University of Rhode Island, where he taught courses on advanced management and consulting skills. He holds the record for selling out the highest-priced workshop at the time (on entrepreneurialism) in the (then) 21-year history of New York City's Learning Annex. His PhD is in psychology.

He is a 2006 inductee into the Professional Speaking Hall of Fame and the concurrent recipient of the National Speakers Association Council of Peers Award of Excellence, representing the top one percent of professional speakers in the world. He is also a Fellow of the Institute of Management Consultants, one of only two people in the world as of this writing holding both honors.

His prolific publishing includes over 500 articles and 45 original books, (and another 10 editions translated into 15 languages), including his best seller, *Million Dollar Consulting* (McGraw-Hill; now in its fifth edition). His newest prior to this one is *Threescore and More* (Taylor and Francis). His books have been on the curricula at Villanova, Temple University, UC Berkeley, and the Wharton School of Business. The Wharton School used his first book, *The Innovation Formula,* in its graduate programs.

He is interviewed and quoted frequently in the media, and his career has taken him to 60 countries and 49 states. (He is afraid to go to North Dakota.) *Success* magazine has cited him in an editorial devoted to his work as "a worldwide expert in executive education." The *New York Post* called him "one of the most highly regarded independent consultants in America." He is the winner of the prestigious Axiem Award for Excellence in Audio Presentation.

In 2006 he was presented with the Lifetime Achievement Award of the American Press Institute, the first ever for a nonjournalist, and one of only seven awarded in the 60-year history of the institute.

He once appeared on the popular American TV game show *Jeopardy!,* where he lost badly in the first round to a dancing waiter from Iowa.

Alan resides in East Greenwich, Rhode Island, with his wife of 50 years, Maria. They have two children, two grandchildren, and two dogs: Bentley, the white German shepherd, and Coco.

Acknowledgments

To Buck, Trotsky, Phoebe, Koufax, Buddy Beagle, Bentley, and Coco.

If anyone requires evidence of God, one need only consider the company of dogs.

Your Mindset Will Determine Your Success

You might be thinking that you're entering a sales job in going out on your own. Or you may believe that the nature of this profession is all about methodology and technology.

Let me disabuse you of such notions right out of the gate.

This is the *marketing* business and you're offering *value* to prospective buyers.

Please assimilate that before you read on. Your mindset is going to determine your success, and I don't mean that in the guise of some bizarre motivational speaker. I mean it as a businessperson who constantly seeks the highest profit with the least labor.

The Notion of Value

This is the *marketing business*. We may be consultants (or coaches, experts, facilitators, trainers, writers, speakers, and so forth) but nevertheless we're in the marketing business. Get used to it.

Marketing is the creation of need. Most people know what they want, but few realize what they need until we propose it to them. If it's strictly what people want that's in question, then the lowest price will often prevail in a commodity competition (lawn mower, computer, consultant). But if you're presenting a unique need they hadn't considered (remote learning, Wi-Fi available in the car, a strategy in six hours), then you are creating something that isn't subject to fee sensitivity.

This is why your mindset must be about the value you bring to the *economic buyer* (the person who can actually approve the check) and not about making a sale. The former is about being willing and eager to approach people because you can help them with your value; the latter is about fear of intruding or being rejected because you are trying to sell—take their money.

It's the difference between giving and taking. I constantly have to reinforce this with even veteran consultants.

When you arise in the morning, you attitude must be, "Another great day to offer people my value," and not, "Another long, slow crawl through enemy territory."

Alanism
Being an expert in the consulting field means focusing on marketing your value to true buyers.

Another benefit of identifying your value is that you won't be intimidated by those who have been around longer, or work for large firms, or who have complex methodologies. I call this pursuit and creation of your personal value the *value proposition*. It can be broad or narrow.

For example, when my clients were primarily Fortune 500 organizations, my value proposition was "I dramatically improve individual and organizational performance." Now that I work with other consultants (actually, the "retail" business), my value proposition is, "I dramatically improve the businesses and lives of entrepreneurs around the world." The value proposition doesn't have to be unique—a lot of people might claim what I've said—but it must represent the initial explanation of the value you convey, the tip of the arrow, so to speak.

So here's your first exercise: Write a one-sentence value proposition below. Try not to use "by," "through," "with," or other prepositions, because they tend to define methodology, not value. Think in terms of results, or: "After I walk away, how is the buyer better off?"

My value proposition:

_____

_____

Digression

Note that my value propositions are very broad. Yours can be quite narrow, such as, "I reduce sales closing time and costs of acquisition." But don't believe the weak advice that you "specialize or die." My 30 years in this business has amply demonstrated that you can "generalize the thrive."

Your value statement needn't be etched in stone, and you may well change it as you proceed through the book. But you have a start, and that's the main thing.

The chart in Figure 1.1 indicates the true power of value as a mind-set. The difference between what a buyer believes is wanted *and what you determine is actually needed* is what I call the *value distance*. The greater the distance, the higher your fee. The smaller the distance, the less your fee, because you're in the commodity sea.

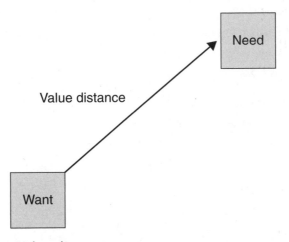

FIGURE 1.1: Value distance.

The final aspect of mindset (for now) is that of your *ideal buyer*. There are still people who contend that everyone is a potential buyer, but that might only occur if your product were oxygen and sunlight, which you'll note are both free. Since you (and I) are lone wolves, we need to focus our precious time and energy on those buyers most likely to say "yes" because they appreciate our value. While others may come our way at times, they are not the ones to whom we should aggressively market.

Thus, the ideal buyer saves us time and energy and maximizes our profits. The ideal buyer is that organizational executive who is most likely to need and appreciate our value. I know it's early, but try to identify that person below (for example, the owner in a small business, the executive director in a nonprofit, the sales vice president or the chief operating officer in a large enterprise):

My ideal buyer:

_____

_____

You can see from Figure 1.2 that the ideal buyer is a slim slice of everyone out there. That's because you're not selling oxygen or sunlight, but rather value not generally available. I call these people "hang tens" in reference to the most aggressive surfers who hang off the front of the board.

Let's move now past your mindset to the mindset of those whom you want around you.

Support Systems

In addition to your own, proper mindset, you'll need the mindsets of others. I'm discussing this prior to office space, bank accounts, insurance, or websites *because all of that is relatively easy, no more than purchase decisions, which can be changed at any time.*

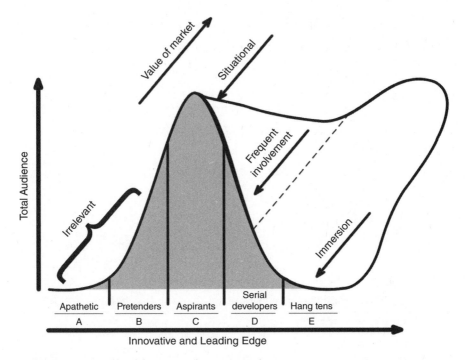

FIGURE 1.2: Ideal buyers (hang tens).

However, there are two issues that will probably spell doom for any solo consultant: one is poor personal relationships, and the other is insufficient funds, and they are obviously inextricably connected. We'll get to the easier of the two—how to make and keep money—a bit later. But let's tackle the critical one first: relationships.

If you have a partner or spouse supportive of your venture you will have a far better chance of success. If you do not have a spouse or partner, then you face some potential obstacles, which we'll deal with below. *But if you have a nonsupportive or even indifferent spouse or partner, you need to attempt to change that now.*

Why would life partners be unsupportive? Here are the reasons:

- You are the sole breadwinner, and they are scared financially since you have less "security" working for yourself.

- They don't understand consulting or solo practice and feel it's impossible to compete against the larger firms.

- You haven't demonstrated any great affinity for sales or marketing.
- Your first few months in the profession have been dismal.
- You've never traveled much alone, and now you'll be away from home more often.

Actually, those are pretty good reasons, right?!

Case in Point

My wife told me early on, "Forget about the mortgage, we'll sell the house if we have to, but you're not going to make any money sitting in your den looking at the phone. Get out of the house!"

Here are my suggestions for enlisting your life partner in the support of your new career:

- Make introductions to successful solo consultants and their partners.
- Explain *how* you expect to compete, generate business, and thrive.
- Have a daily debriefing on progress—good, bad, and ugly. (We've always done this over dinner.)
- Show the total cash reserves you have available: bank accounts, credit lines, retirement funds, investments, securities, refinancing potential, and so forth. You may never need them, but they're there, and no one is going to debtor's prison.
- Have your partner read this book. Show that there is a rational approach to being successful and that thousands have done so.

All of these steps should dramatically improve the relationship aspects of your new career. But if you are experiencing relationship problems for other reasons, going out on your own will almost always exacerbate them. Reconcile them first, one way or another, before embarking on a path that requires loving support.

What if you don't have a partner? Well, then you need to create a support system. These *are not* business or professional advisors per se. In other words, not necessarily your attorney or accountant (although they might fit the bill if they're also personal friends).

Alanism

In this business you need someone to commiserate with the lows and celebrate the highs, but most of all, to keep you honest with yourself.

Here are typical people to recruit into your support system:[1]

- Other solo consultants who don't directly compete
- Colleagues in trade and professional associations as well as in social clubs
- Community leaders, perhaps from the chamber of commerce, Rotary, and so forth
- Family members who you know are supportive and not envious or overly critical
- Independent business owners in other enterprises who can empathize
- Long-term, understanding friends

How big should your support system be? Who knows? Just remember that the purpose is to enable you to have a sounding board for your ideas and to interpret your successes and failures, and to keep you centered. In other words, one rejection from a prospect doesn't make you a lousy marketer, and one signed contract doesn't make you a superstar.

The support team needn't be gathered, or meet, or even know each other. This isn't a group to which you report. It is a group composed of individuals who can listen well and provide you with objective feedback. Otherwise, *you'll spend immense amounts of time worrying about insignificant matters, trying to interpret the vague utterances of prospects, and generally indulging in too much introspection!*

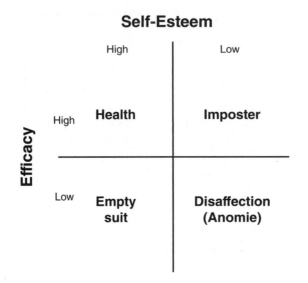

FIGURE 1.3: Self-esteem and efficacy.

What we do isn't rocket science. But what we do is extremely personal and can too often be perceived as commentary on our *self-worth*. In Figure 1.3 you can see the importance of perspective.

When we're good at what we do (efficacious) and also feel good about ourselves, we are emotionally healthy. But when we don't feel worthy, even though we're successful by other metrics, we believe that we're imposters and about to be found out.[2]

Many people who are good at what they do don't believe they deserve it, creating the "imposter" syndrome in the upper right of the chart. This has been found among business executives, performers, athletes, and politicians. When you feel like an imposter ("Why would they believe what I'm telling them?"), you're subject to rapid decompression when someone does challenge you ("I've been found out!"). In this context, you may be effective, but you feel unworthy, so a critique quickly reinforces those inferiority feelings.

The converse is the "empty suit," who has feelings of great self-worth but not much talent. This is the person who can talk a good game (in Texas: "Big hat, no cattle") yet doesn't deliver on the talk.

And if you're weak in both self-worth and effectiveness, you are alienated and disaffected, odd person out. There's a type of suicide called

"anomic suicide," which is caused when someone feels completely alienated from those around him or her, is unable to perform well, and feels worthless.

Your support systems are intended to keep you focused with honest, tough-love feedback and support, so that the lows are never catastrophic, and the highs are never too euphoric.

When you're getting started in consulting, this is especially critical.

Basic Necessities

Let's move now from your fundamental, positive mindset to what will support that mindset in your daily life. This section is about the physical assets you need at the outset to bolster your positive intent.

Office

You don't need an office. What you need is a quiet place where you can work undisturbed, meaning you need a door and room for a desk and chair with Wi-Fi access.

When I began consulting on my own, after I was fired in 1985, my wife talked me out of an office, explaining that if it turned out I needed one I could get one later. I never did need one, using instead a spare bedroom converted for my purposes. I figured out that I saved, over 16 years, $450,000 in rent, insurance, utilities, maintenance, repairs, and furnishings. And $450,000 is almost *exactly what it cost me to put my two kids through 16 years of private school with no indebtedness on their shoulders when they were graduated from college*!

You home office is deductible under the tax laws in effect as I write this.[3] And you can pay yourself rent, deducting also the expenses for your house represented by the percentage of space occupied by your office (for example, insurance, mortgage costs, and the like).

Alanism
The more comfortable you are and the more professional you feel, the more productive you will be. That's very tough with an ironing board or litter box in the room.

Stock your office with:

- Normal supplies (copy paper, stapler, tape, markers, and so forth)
- Postage meter (leased from Pitney Bowes, usually)[4]
- Copier that can also serve as a scanner and fax machine (yes, some people still fax)
- Computer of your choice
- Alexa, or an equivalent music and information source
- Ergonomic chair
- Paintings or photos on the walls that please you
- Phone system that can be used for conferencing, has a backup voice mail function, and has a speaker (ideally two lines, house and office; cells are fine but awkward for long calls)

If you don't have such room, then consider a shared-suite provider. These operations charge a monthly fee for a receptionist, offices of varying sizes, office equipment, shared copiers, and so forth. Many will also serve as a mail drop and answering service.

What should guide your choice is privacy. You shouldn't be in a place in your home with a heavy traffic pattern, ambient noise, or distractions. (You need to tell your family that when the door is closed, you're out of town.) A home office can be a blessing or a curse, depending on your level of discipline. I've coached too many people who never got around to calling for referrals because they kept staring at a guitar in the corner wondering if they could master a diminished fifth chord.

Basically, your office should make you happy to be there (natural light helps tremendously). The degree to which it's complete as a resource for you will be determined by how often you have to leave it to perform tasks. The fewer occasions, the better.

Professional Help

You'll need the following from the outset:

- *Attorney.* This shouldn't be your cousin Louie or the person who closed on your mortgage. You need someone who can create your company bylaws, help trademark intellectual property (the marks™ and®), and create and/or review client contracts. Your attorney will also provide for incorporating your business, and with your accountant will advise (under current laws) whether you're best off financially being a C corporation, Subchapter S, or LLC.

- *Insurance agent or broker.* You *must* carry what's called *E&O* (*errors and omissions*) *insurance,* colloquially known as "malpractice insurance"). This is a litigious society, *and some clients will demand proof of such coverage before hiring you.* You'll also need liability insurance, which covers you if someone trips over the power cord connected to your laptop at a meeting (even if someone else connected it). E&O can be about $2,500 annually (at the moment, for about a million dollars in coverage), but liability is inexpensive. You should also carry your own life insurance, health insurance, disability insurance, and umbrella liability insurance. This is why you need a good broker.[5]

- *Bookkeeper.* This is the person who takes your checkbook stubs, receipts, and bank statements and creates a monthly profit and loss statement, a general ledger, and the inputs for your tax people. I strongly advise you to pay someone to do this (probably about $200 to $300 per month) rather than attempt to do it yourself using software, even if you're a financial consultant. Have independent eyes and calculators do this.

- *Tax professionals.* The tax laws have more pages than the combined constitutions of the world's democracies, so let the professionals figure out your taxes. The government takes a very dim few of errors on returns and claims of honest mistakes.

- *Payroll services.* Use Paychex or a similar resource to pay your salary, withhold taxes, and file electronic reports. Do *not* attempt to get a check weekly or monthly of a certain amount. These services enable you to tell them the size of check you want and the withholding amounts, so that you can receive cash from your company based on your actual expenses and needs.

Do not use or hire the following:

- Services that promise you leads every month.
- SEO (search engine optimization) services that promise greater visibility on the web.
- Any coach who hasn't done what you want to do successfully. A coaching certificate from some group means absolutely zero. (Who certifies the certifiers?)
- Services that promise you networking opportunities.
- Services that claim you'll be a speaker in front of buyers if you pay them a fee.
- Anyone who offers a cable TV or AM radio show if you pay for it.
- Anyone who offers a celebrity to appear with you on video if you pay for it. (The "celebrities" usually are D-list or so ancient that someone has to prop them up or they'll fall over.)

Stationery, Literature, and So On: Hard and Soft

This is an electronic age, yet we still don't have a checkless society or a paperless office. You will need a business card to hand out, which should have your name, title, business name, phone, physical address, and email address. This isn't an advertising billboard, though some clueless consultants think it's clever to put promotional wording on the back or their photo on the front. Picture your buyers, with whom you should be a peer. Do they have their photos and excess verbiage on their cards?

Similarly, have hard copy letterhead. You will sometimes need to send a hard copy letter, so you'll need envelopes and address labels. When you start out, have a local artist, or even art student, create a logo for you to place on your website, stationery, card, and so on. You can always change it later, but it will add professionalism from the outset.

Virtually everything else can be virtual. You don't need a sophisticated website at the outset, but you need a home page that provides these items, which we'll tackle in detail later in the book:

- Typical client results
- Video and text testimonials
- Your photo
- How best to reach you[6]

We'll talk about blogs, more website content, newsletters, and so forth as we proceed. But for now, these are the essentials to put in place.

Hitting the Ground Running

The final major factor in mindset is to gain momentum early. You can begin this before you leave your current position (remember that most of us are refugees from larger organizations). I'm sure you can see the obvious: set up your office, arrange for incorporation, purchase insurance, print stationery, and so forth.

However, here are eight less obvious ways to stack the deck and support your mindset:

1. If you are currently employed and leaving amicably, explore a consulting relationship with your soon-to-be-ex-employer, which might cover some of the work you currently do more efficiently and less expensively than hiring a replacement.

2. Make a list of everyone you know, and put each one into one of three categories:

   A. Those likely to be buyers or recommenders

   B. Those about whom you're uncertain

   C. Those you're sure are neither

For example, your dentist or attorney should be in category A, since they will clearly have clients to whom they can refer you.

3. Seek to meet other consultants who would be willing to share with you what they did well and not so well in starting their own practices. Make sure they are successful people. There can be far too much "big hat, no cattle" in this profession.

4. Prepare your family. Let your family know what to expect. You may be traveling; you can't be disturbed when the office door is closed; there's a phone line they shouldn't answer; you may be able to be at a dance recital or soccer game in the middle of the day; you may be able to include some vacation time with business trips if they come along. Be sure to include these positives with the negatives.

5. Look for inexpensive associations to join. The chamber of commerce may make sense. There may be a consulting organization with a local chapter. If possible, private clubs make sense, since many of your prospective buyers will be members. And charities and community group are important because they're always looking for volunteers, and your buyers will often be on the board or major donors. (If there's a local theater or dance group, just look at the donors, who are usually listed in the playbill.)

6. Study the craft. I strongly recommend that you read these books as far in advance of your start as you can:

The Capitalist Philosophers, by Andrea Gabor: A quick history of consulting and the major thought leaders therein.

Innovation and Entrepreneurship, by Peter Drucker: He literally invented modern strategy while working for William Sloane at General Motors.

Million Dollar Consulting, by Alan Weiss: I've written more books on consulting than anyone in history, and this is the *magnum opus*, on the shelves for over a quarter century through five editions.

These three books are a great start and will generate still more options for you.

7. Put your financial house in order. Ideally, you should have at least six months of normal expenses set aside as you begin this journey. I've found that disciplined people can usually make a first sale within six months and begin to support their regular lifestyles in 12. Specifically, do the following:

   • Identify all of your assets.

   • Determine which will initially fund your business if you're not receiving severance or money from other sources.

   • Determine reserve funding sources—for example, invested retirement funds.[7]

   • Calculate what the total available credit is on your credit cards and other lines of credit (for example, second mortgage).

   > **Alanism**
   > It neither illegal nor unethical to prepare for your own future while living in someone else's present.

   • Ask yourself how comfortable you (and your spouse) would be borrowing money from family members who could afford to make such loans.

   The idea here is not to build a huge cash pile by exhausting these sources. Rather, it's to build the mindset that you're not about to go broke, you don't need to make a sale tomorrow, and you have far more resources than you might think. When you go into your own business, there is no such thing as untouchable money!

8. Create your business checking and savings accounts. Work with a bank that can provide you with the ability to send and accept wire funds, and set up a merchant account to receive payments (Mastercard, Visa, Amex, Diners Club) and electronic banking to move funds around 24/7.

Case in Point

Pay yourself from every incoming transaction. In other words, if you receive a payment from a client for $25,000, put $2,500 of it in a savings account and the balance in the checking account. If you are disciplined in doing this, you'll build up a nice cash reserve. Don't even worry about the interest rates; just put the money aside.

The idea in this chapter has been preparation, to some extent physically, but to a larger extent mentally and emotionally. *Logic makes you think, but it's emotion that makes you act.* That's true of clients and true of all of us.

Figure 1.4 shows the basic progression that we'll be working through in terms of securing business.

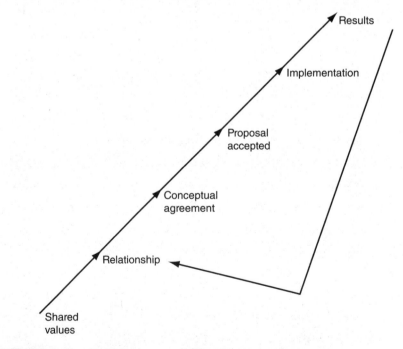

FIGURE 1.4: Business acquisition progression.

We are searching for prospects with whom we can work ethically (shared values), build a trusting relationship, agree on outcomes, submit a proposal, implement the project, and then obtain the results that further cements the relationship and creates expanded business and referral business.

The right mindset is how to get started getting started.

Chapter 1 Definitions

Economic buyer: A business executive who can sign or authorize a check to pay for your value—as opposed to lower-level people (gatekeepers) who can say "no" but cannot say "yes."

Marketing: The creation of need. The more that need is unique to your value, the easier to acquire business that is not fee sensitive.

Value: The improvement delivered through the consultant's actions and involvement. This can be tangible (money saved) or intangible (a heightened sense of well-being).

Value proposition: A one-sentence "tip of the arrow" explanation of how people's conditions are improved by having worked with you.

Value distance: The range from what the buyer wants to what you determine the buyer actually needs, creating a uniqueness about you and higher fee potential.

Ideal buyer: That economic buyer who is most likely to appreciate your particular value more than all other buyers.

Self-worth: Confidence in one's abilities and intentions through both victories and defeats.

Malpractice (E&O) insurance: Covers you in case you're sued for providing poor advice in the client's opinion that cost the client money and material damage.

Notes

1. You *do not* need a board or advisory group of any kind. The last thing you need in going out on your own is to create bureaucratic oversight!

2. This is why movie actors, with an award in their hands, still worry about whether they'll ever work again, because they've been given an award for portraying someone other than themselves. (My son and daughter are in the business.)

3. Consult a good lawyer and put the provision in your company bylaws. The historical IRS criteria have been that the space is used solely for your business, you have no other place of business, and you are the sole user.

4. You can use various online stamp sources, but I've found a personal scale and meter a great deal easier.

5. Some of these items can be paid with company funds, pretax, depending on your bylaws, which is why you need a good attorney.

6. Always include a physical address. Some people need to mail you things, such as checks or packages. It's amateurish not to have a physical address because you're concerned about security. Rent a postal box if that makes you more comfortable.

7. Under current laws, IRA and similar withdrawals may be made without tax liability if they are redeposited within 60 days—an interest-free loan.

Chapter

Barging into the Business

There is no reason to crawl into this business. In fact, there are virtually no barriers to entry. When I wrote the original editions of my classic *Million Dollar Consulting*[1] in 1992, I found, to my astonishment, that there was far more licensing required to be a palm reader on the boardwalk at Atlantic City than there was to put up a consulting shingle! That hasn't changed.

So why not hit the ground zooming?

The Concept of Marketing Gravity

There are two ways to engage with prospects:

1. Go find them.
2. Allow them to find you.

The second way is far less expensive and time consuming. But, in starting in this profession, how can you attract people to your value (not your "work")?

As you'll see in Figure 2.1, there are a great many ways to attract people. Not all of them will be appropriate for you, so you have to choose what's in your comfort zone at first and broaden the choices later. (If none of these is in your comfort zone and never will be, then I'd suggest you stop reading here and pick up *Getting Started in Actuarial Work* or *Getting Started in Construction*.)

These days, with instant and mass virtual communications, *marketing gravity* is enabled more than ever. But you have to be selective and unique. None of us buys from the spammers who send out global email blasts for rising to the top of Google listings. We automatically delete such annoyances.

So, our job is to be compelling and not annoying.

Let's go around the wheel from the 12 o'clock position.

Pro bono work. This can be so important for those new to the profession that we'll discuss it in a following segment in this chapter separately.

FIGURE 2.1: Marketing gravity components.

Commercial publishing. A book is a business card on steroids. It's never too early to write a book, and I encourage people to write one every two years, at least. I'm still doing so on a yearly basis. A commercial publisher (meaning you're being paid for your talent, as opposed to a vanity press, where you pay them) becomes a third-party endorser of your work, believing you are important enough to merit an investment in your work.

Position papers. These are brief (two to six pages) statements of your stance on certain business issues. For example, you might write a position paper (sometimes called a "white paper") titled "How to Provide Nonfinancial Incentives" or "Creating a Mentoring System within Your Organization." The point here is to provide value to the reader that prompts follow-up and inquiry with you. These papers can be repurposed into some of the other gravity options below. Always place your *copyright* symbol (©) on the paper.[2]

Radio interviews. These are almost always done from your home by phone and average 10 to 30 minutes. They are based on your latest *intellectual property* (*IP*), book, or articles. There are companies that create these for you for a fee (for example, 20 interviews for $3,500) but you can start in your local area by contacting the producers (not the hosts) of local talk radio shows. Listen to the show first so you can make a compelling argument as to why what you have to contribute is important for that particular audience.

TV appearances. I'd like to basically tell you what *not* to do first in this category. *Never* accept an offer to appear on a TV show with some ancient celebrity or D-list personality for a fee. No one watches these, and everyone knows you're paying to be there. There are firms that will place you on TV, radio, or in print on a pay-for-play basis (as noted above), meaning you pay them when it actually happens. But more simply at the start, try to meet the local TV producers, anchors, and reporters on a networking basis, or send them items of interest for their reports.

You're more likely to be successful at this in smaller markets (Providence, Kansas City, Denver) than in larger ones (New York, Chicago, Los Angeles).

Advertising. This doesn't work in terms of newspaper ads or billboards. But it *can* work when targeted. For example, if you specialize in selling dental practices, advertise in a newsletter from the American Dental Association. If you're a small-business expert, advertise in the local weekly business periodical. For example, in the church bulletin distributed at Mass, there is always a page or two devoted to people's ads that are relevant for parishioners, from real estate to snowplowing, from financial advice to business coaching.

Passive listings. When you belong to an organization, such as the chamber of commerce, or when you donate to an organization, such as a local theater or hospital, your name will appear on the appropriate lists of members or donors. If you use your company name, and it's descriptive (for example, Jones Business Growth Consulting, Inc.), you gain visibility.

Speaking. This is a major gravitational force that can justify an entire book on the field alone.[3] Don't worry about your speaking fee for now; speak for free *if you have buyers in the room.* This is an ideal opportunity to demonstrate your expertise and meeting people who can purchase it. Practice with local community groups or a Toastmasters chapter.

Website. A website is *not* a sales tool, but rather a *credibility* tool. You don't need an elaborate one to begin. I've included it in marketing gravity because it can convince others of your worth. Ask others who have begun their practices (in any field) recently who they use for the design work. Don't choose random people from email spam or web lists. You can pay by the hour, and at the outset you simple need a home landing page with your logo, typical client results, and some testimonials.[4] On another page you can have a description of your services. Start simple, ignore the promotion of SEO (which is irrelevant in this business), and build it slowly and inexpensively.

Electronic newsletters. Start one once you have about 100 names on your lists. They can be very brief—a paragraph or two—and should address topics within your expertise that are valuable and provocative. Use an ISSN number[5] and either your own computer software (e.g., Constant Contact) or a *listserv* to send it out. The key here is to be absolutely consistent—every Monday morning, or the first of every month, and so forth.

Word of mouth. The research today and for the past dec-ade has shown that executive buyers use peer reference and word of mouth more than any other source for mak-ing buying decisions.[6] In the corporate world, overwhelm-ingly, decisions are made by listening to trusted others. (How do you tend to choose a vacation destination, car dealer, or doctor? You ask friends or authorities.) Try to attend events and use your current contacts to spread the words about your business ven-ture, value, quality, *and results for your clients.*

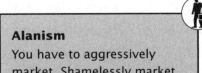

Alanism
You have to aggressively market. Shamelessly market. If you don't blow your own horn, there is no music.

Trade association leadership. There are a variety of groups you can join, from the content focus of your consulting (e.g., in retail, manufacturing, financial services, transportation, etc.) to process organizations (coaching, consulting, facilitating, speaking, and others). If you join such organizations, try to assume a leadership role (e.g., chair of recruiting, or treasurer, or program director) where possible. Don't merely be a member of the herd.

Third-party endorsements. There's a reason you see forewords by well-known experts and endorsements on books. They help to sell books. These days a one-minute video, even shot casually by a client or referral source, attesting to your value and expertise and posted on your site, can go a long way to accelerating your business prospects.

Referrals. These are the lifeblood of any business, new or veteran, and we'll discuss them in greater depth in the following section.

Print newsletters. Yes, we've been in an electronic age for some time, but that's why a hard copy letter often gets more attention than email, and it's why a hard copy newsletter may acquire more attention than an attachment to email. Keep it short, use visuals and photos, and maintain a disciplined schedule. We all regularly receive such traditional mailings from financial experts, real estate experts, and health sources because they can stand out in an otherwise electronic crowd.

Print interviews. In addition to the tactics mentioned above under radio and TV interviews, write to the business editor of local newspapers and business publications and suggest a meeting to explore ideas you have for articles and columns—and for an interview. If they can't or won't meet, then send them examples. Also, write to reporters who have published relevant articles for your practice, compliment them on their work (important!), and then provide still more information about the topic, using your expertise. It's likely you may become a source.

Teaching. Edgar Schein, the superb authority on consulting, once commented that "if you want to learn something, try to teach it." Look for opportunities in university extension courses, or in night school programs, or junior colleges. You can be a visiting lecturer or guest speaker. This also raises your visibility and exposure.

Alliances. These are rare but can be effective, especially at the outset. You may be able to find an alliance partner in a noncompetitive firm (such as legal, accounting, design, and so forth) where there is a win/win/win dynamic. You provide your value in a presentation or meeting, your alliance partners have the benefit of introducing that value to their customers, and the customers walk away with new skills and learning. You, of course, have them now as prospects. You can also do this with a private social club (such as the university clubs found in many cities), which often have enrichment series for members and whose presenters don't have to be members.

Products. Having products—especially electronic products such as ebooks—is a great way to attract people to your offerings, obtain email addresses, and build some repute. Although you should put a price on the books, manuals, downloads, and so forth, you will mostly give them away for free to gain attention for your work. (We'll discuss "passive income" in Chapter 10.)

Networking. Like referrals, this is an approach with its own integrity and structure, and we'll address it later in this chapter.

Marketing gravity has a lot of "spokes," and you don't have to adopt or be comfortable with all of them. In fact, few people are. But you need to utilize four or five on a regular, disciplined, organized basis when you launch your practice or firm in order to draw people to you and build your brand.

If none of these is attractive to you, then that's okay—so long as you go into another line of work.

Calling Everyone You Know

As promised, this segment deals with referrals, and how to systematically mine them for introductions and business, something you should do throughout your career, and something that even veterans don't always do correctly or frequently enough.

As a newcomer to the profession, whether this is a second career or a first career, here is how to get referral business as rapidly as possible:

1. Make a list of everyone you know:
   • Past business relationships
   • Social friends

- Extended family
- Professional resources (doctors, attorneys, and so forth)
- Colleagues (in professional associations)
- Colleagues (in community groups and charities)
- Alumni
- Club members (social or athletic)

Don't exclude anyone; just list names. A spreadsheet helps tremendously.

2. Separate the list into three (probably unequal) categories:

    A. Those you suspect or know would be buyers or recommenders of your value.

    B. Those you're not sure if they're buyers or recommenders.

    C. Those you're sure are neither.

3. Call everyone in category A. Do this so that it's not onerous: perhaps one or two a day, five to ten a week. Do not email; call. If you get voice mail leave the message below, which you should deliver to the person when you reach him or her:

> *Joan, this is Stuart Mills, and I'm engaged in an exciting new venture, which has gained quite a bit of interest. I would love to get 20 minutes in person to obtain your guidance and reactions about where I should be headed with my plans.*

The idea here is:

- Scheduling a small amount of time requested, not burdensome.
- Setting up personal meeting (Skype or Zoom if they're too distant).
- Determining if they personally might wish to hire you.
- Gaining referrals to others who may wish to hire you.

Always keep in mind the mindset that we explored at the outset of this book: you're providing value, not selling, and you're trying to make that value available to as many appropriate people as you can. When you ask who might be interested from whom they know (the referral), try to suggest people by name ("What about Zack Taylor?") or position ("How about your former boss at the insurance company?").

4. Write an email to the same effect to everyone in category B. However, personalize it so that it's not seen as a mass mailing:

> *Tony, it's been six months since we last spoke. Did your daughter successfully choose a college to attend? I'm writing because I'm engaged in an exciting new venture, which has gained quite a bit of interest. I would love to get 20 minutes in person to obtain your guidance and reactions about where I should be headed with my plans.*

Follow up only with those who write back positively.

5. Do nothing special with category C, but put all three categories on your mailing list. (See the importance of lists in the "Marketing Gravity" section above. Simply give people the opt-out ability on subsequent mailings.)

If you do this with discipline—literally call everyone you know—you'll develop business and leads far more rapidly, sometimes within 30 days. But you must be assiduous about this. It must be done every week. (And when you've achieved a successful career, even then all contacts should be renewed once a quarter.)

Making Money by Working for Free (Pro Bono)

As a newcomer to the profession, it's vitally important to make contacts with the movers and shakers who can accelerate your growth and increase your visibility. In Figure 2.1, pro bono work is at the 12 o'clock position.

Never work for free for a for-profit, as a rule. But here's when working for free can make a huge difference.

Find a charity, arts group, or some other nonprofit and volunteer your *professional* services (don't simply become a volunteer). If your expertise is in acquiring talent, offer to help to recruit volunteers. If it's in strategy, offer to run some strategy sessions. Approach the executive director and say, "To pay back the community I engage in two pro bono projects a year, and I thought you might like to discuss one here." Keep it to 60–90 days on a part-time basis, and ask for a testimonial when you're done. This will hugely increase your visibility and also introduce you to major donors and board members, many of whom may be your buyers or recommenders.

It's important to take the position that you do this a couple of times a year and that it's your contribution to the cause and the community, *not* an attempt by you to meet people to whom you can market! That's why you need:

- A cause you truly support and admire
- A substantial enough operation to have a board of directors, major donors, and community stature
- An executive director or CEO who is accessible and is clearly the buyer
- An organization with needs commensurate to your skills and value
- A short-term project (60–90 days) with clear objectives and metrics of success

For example, if your value is talent acquisition and retention, perhaps the organization needs help recruiting volunteers. If your expertise is strategy, perhaps you can facilitate a board retreat.

Make sure you can arrange the following:

- Meet with the board members individually.
- Create some media coverage, press releases, and so forth.
- Obtain a testimonial when the project is successfully completed.
- The ability to cite the organization as one with which you've worked.[7]

Someone I coached performed pro bono work for a local YMCA and wound up with a paid project at YMCAs across the country. As an exception to my rule about not working free for a for-profit, another delivered a half day on innovation to a 12-person insurance brokerage and wound up with a full-fee keynote for the parent organization (the local brokerage manager was on the programming committee for the national convention). A third did a lunch-and-learn session for HBO in New York and acquired a project with the finance department whose vice president happened to be attending the session. (These are free lunchtime sessions for any employees who choose to attend.)

The key here is twofold: First, you want to do great work and impress all those who meet you, and also those who learn of your work with the organization. Second, you want to follow up, at a later date, with key people you met who may be buyers and recommenders.

Nonprofits usually love the help, and this is an excellent marketing gravity method to meet people and attract others to you.

Networking Is a Process, Not an Event

Networking is one of those potentially highly effective techniques that's almost always done incorrectly. This is *not* an event at which you collect business cards or glad-hand everyone in sight. It's the beginning of a *process* of meeting key buyers and recommenders.

I've created a five-step process to help make this methodical, repeatable, and utterly reliable:

1. *Distance power.* You're better off networking with strangers than with people who know you even slightly. Those who know you will have some impression, usually not consistent with your new career. You're better off starting at square zero with people who don't know you at all.

2. *The unique multiplier.* There are people who are not buyers but who know *a lot of buyers.* Making that one acquaintance at a networking event is hugely important, since you'll achieve many contacts as a result.

3. *The nexus person.* This is someone who knows one true buyer. The words used are usually "You need to meet my uncle (brother, father, son, cousin, daughter, and so forth), who could really use your help."

4. *Reciprocity.* You have to give to get. If you meet the head of a search firm whose clients might be appropriate for your consulting expertise, offer to provide his or her name to other people you know who may need to hire talent. If you meet the editor of the local newspaper who might feature your work, give the editor insights into some potential news stories in your town.

5. *The contextual connection.* Remember that you are a peer of the person you're seeking to meet by dint of both supporting the same cause that brings you together at this event.

Networking is a process, not an event. You are trying to set up subsequent meetings with someone who can buy from you or recommend you to buyers. Don't try to sell at the event; simply establish a connection and a reason to contact that person subsequently. Never hand things out that people have to carry around! Even your business card isn't important—it's more important to get the other person's and an agreement that you can call them on a specific date and time.

Network in neutral gatherings: charity fundraisers, political rallies, awards ceremonies, community meetings, arts groups, and so forth. When you meet someone, determine if they might be a buyer or recommender by asking why they're attending the event and what their

Alanism

After any meeting with a buyer or recommender, *always* establish a subsequent action, date, and time. Never accept, "Give me a call in a couple of weeks." Say, I'll call you on the ninth at 10 on your cell phone."

occupation is. If they seem to be buyers, engage them briefly with some value or insights:

> **Buyer:** I'm the senior vice president of lending for Acme Bank.
>
> **You:** I'm a customer! I saw that you're looking for more help in the branch I use.
>
> **Buyer:** That's probably true; we have a staffing shortage that's pretty critical.
>
> **You:** I specialize in talent attraction and retention. This isn't the time or the place, but I'd love to give you some ideas from my other clients. Are you available later this week?
>
> **Buyer:** I'm not, but I'm back on Monday.
>
> **You:** Why don't we meet for 30 minutes this Monday? What's a good time for you, and what number should I use to confirm?

It's as simple as that.

Getting started in consulting requires that kind of assertiveness and confidence. So long as you believe you're providing value, there's nothing holding you back from barging into the business.

Chapter 2 Definitions

Marketing gravity: The compelling elements you employ to attract economic buyers to you.

Intellectual property (IP): Those ideas, models, visuals, and arguments that are original to you and provide the potential for others to learn and perform better.

Copyright: The legal protection for your original ideas in writing, speech, and other forms that is automatically in place but that is best reflected with a copyright line.

(continued)

> **Listserv:** A service that maintains your mailing lists and enables you to easily mail to some or all of the names whenever desired or automatically at set intervals.
>
> **Networking:** The act of meeting people at various events with the purpose of obtaining subsequent contact to obtain business or referrals to buyers.

Notes

1. *Million Dollar Consulting* (McGraw-Hill, 1992).

2. Anything that is originally yours is automatically copyrighted. You use either "Copyright Alan Weiss 2019" or "© Alan Weiss 2019," but never both. You do not need to send a copy to the commissioner of patents, sometimes recommended by others but totally unnecessary and time consuming.

3. And I wrote it: *Million Dollar Speaking* (McGraw-Hill, 2011).

4. Don't have any clients yet? Get character testimonials from those who know you who have business titles.

5. An International Standard Serial Number, used to distinguish and easily find your newsletter. You can obtain it here: https://www.loc.gov/issn.

6. See, for example, *Invisible Influence* by Jonah Berger (Simon & Schuster, 2017).

7. If you're making a speech within the organization or on their behalf, get permission to videotape it.

Chapter

Becoming a Marketer

arketing to me is the creation and accentuation of need for your ideal customers, which allows you do provide products and services for them that fulfill such need. There is strategic marketing (Ford advertising about the quality of its trucks nationally) and tactical marketing (a local Ford dealer promoting a special sale on the coming weekend). The former builds the brand; the latter focuses on the actual sale.

Creating an Accelerant Curve

I've created a dynamic called the "accelerant curve," which will help you from the outset determine the products and services to provide for your ideal clients. (See Figure 1.2 in Chapter 1 for a reminder.) The purpose is to create a marketing sequence that attracts prospects, prompts them to move into various buying options, and continues to move them into unique, high-fee, low-labor relationships with you.

By building your accelerant curve early (and it's always a work in progress) you can save enormous amounts of time and energy by focusing on the key products and services to best develop for your ideal buyers (who may change over time, which is why this is an organic work in progress).

Alanism

Your value proposition, identification of your ideal buyer, creation of marketing gravity options, and the development of your accelerant curve constitute your marketing plan. You don't need a business plan— you're not Apple.

Let's examine what this might look like for you.

The premise of the accelerant curve is to offer free or low-cost aspects of your value to draw people to you (left side of Figure 3.1) and then move them down the curve to higher value and more expensive offerings. The ultimate position is the "vault" on the right, which is high income, low labor, and uniquely you.

On the left (which is basically "competitive" with others) you may choose to offer:

- Newsletters
- Teleconferences
- Podcasts
- Blog posts
- Booklets and ebooks
- Videos
- Informal breakfasts with peer groups

As you move toward the center (labeled "distinctive") you may be offering:

- Coaching
- Workshops
- Basic project consulting
- Facilitation
- Retreats

On the right ("breakthrough") you might offer:

- Long-term project oversight
- Sophisticated coaching for executives
- Complex consulting projects

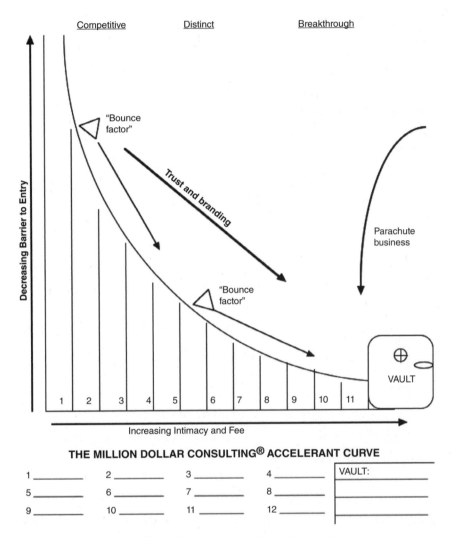

Competitive   Distinct   Breakthrough

THE MILLION DOLLAR CONSULTING® ACCELERANT CURVE

1 _____	2 _____	3 _____	4 _____	VAULT:
5 _____	6 _____	7 _____	8 _____	_____
9 _____	10 _____	11 _____	12 _____	_____

FIGURE 3.1: The Million Dollar Consulting® accelerant curve.

- Strategy sessions
- M&A (merger and acquisition) assistance
- Operational audits
- Talent management

In the vault, as you progress, you can develop and offer:

- Trusted advisor services
- Destination events

- Mentoring
- Innovation consulting

I've tried to be generic in my examples. You should adjust these to your expertise. If your expertise were sales, then:

- *Competitive.* Free sales video on closing techniques
- *Distinctive.* Coaching on the assumptive close technique
- *Breakthrough.* Sales strategies for global customers
- *Vault.* Creating evangelism, where customers sell for you

Along the way are "bounce factors," which propel clients further down the curve at a faster pace. For example, many people who, like you, are reading this book, have read my book *Million Dollar Consulting*, which sells for about $16, and then enrolled in my Million Dollar Consulting® College, a multiday, in-depth vault item that costs $16,000. It's that direct.

"Parachute business" occurs when someone hears about you (typically because of a strong brand) and enters the vault immediately, without going through the curve. The right side of the curve is what I consider "breakthrough."

You don't need the 12 offerings we've just described, but *you do need offerings across the spectrum.* And they needn't be wildly different. You can offer remote coaching on the left, a month of personal coaching on site in the middle, and in-depth coaching involving 360° assessments and shadowing on the right.[1] In the vault, you could offer long-term support as a trusted advisor in your field.

The important aspect here is to understand that you need a *process* that uses marketing gravity with ideal buyers to place them on your accelerant curve. Before we move on, write down just two offerings that you can create now or in the near future for each of the dynamics. These will change as you become more expert and develop a more powerful brand, but even at this point they will help you to understand how to treat prospects, and then treat new clients, and eventually even mature clients.

Left (Competitive)

1. _____

2. _____

Middle (Distinctive)

1. _____

2. _____

Right (Breakthrough)

1. _____

2. _____

Vault

1. _____

2. _____

Now let's consider a way to make money *and to market* at the same time in the same place.

Money Talks

One of the best places to impress buyers in on stage. As soon as you can, find places where you can speak for free at first. Don't worry about not having a speaking background, if that's the case, because for now you're doing this for free, using your expertise to help others, and also demonstrating to them that you can be an important resource.

Where might you speak for free?

- Rotary and other service clubs
- Private club enrichment events (you don't have to be a member)
- Chambers of commerce
- Local operations of larger institutions[2]
- Charities (United Way, Red Cross, March of Dimes)
- Arts groups (theater, dance, music)
- Community events (awards ceremonies, political rallies)
- Lunch-and-learn sessions (companies offer lunchtime education)
- Library events
- College extension programs
- Convention or visitor's bureau programs[3]

The point of doing this is at least fourfold:

1. Improve your visibility and your repute.
2. Hone your skills in low-pressure environments.
3. Meet the audience both onstage and off (networking).
4. Meet the organizers, donors, and board members.

Once you develop comfort in speaking and taking questions, you can look for opportunities at trade associations, professional associations, and company conferences. I suggest that you develop a fee schedule along these lines early in your career, raising the fees as you gain repute and confidence:

- Keynote (60–90 minutes): $5,000
- Workshop (half day): $7,500
- Seminar (full day): $9,000

You can provide a discount if there are multiple days involved. This is meant only as a guide, but also as a warning to not set your fees too low. People believe they get what they pay for. At this writing, the highest noncelebrity fees (people not known well outside of their specialty or industry) are about $35,000 for a keynote. Even celebrities—for example, authors of well-received books—are in the $40,000 to $60,000 range in most cases.

As you are reading this, organizations all around the country and around the world are holding meetings with speakers from the outside (mostly paid). Here are some resources and routes to gain entry into this marketplace:

- *Toastmasters.* This is a fine boot camp to learn basic speaking in a supportive atmosphere in local chapters. Though they hold all kinds of competitions and award prizes, it's an amateur's organization. If you're good, you'll outgrow it, and don't make the mistake of lingering here too long. But it's a fine launch platform. Toastmasters International: —https://www.toastmasters.org.

- *National Speakers Association.* This is a group for professional speakers (that is, those intent on making paid speeches) who either are solely speakers (increasingly rare) or are using speaking to market themselves while being paid for their efforts. They have local chapters and national conventions, as well as monthly publications. They, too, provide accolades and honorifics, but these are irrelevant in the world of the true buyer. However, you'll meet peers and especially learn stage mechanics and comfort. National Speakers Association: https://www.nsaspeaker.org; Global Speakers Federation: https://www.asiaspeakers.org/global.

- *National Trade and Professional Associations of the United States.* This is a hard-copy book and electronic resource that provides the names of the approximately 10,000 trade and professional associations in the United States, the name of the executive director, their budget and membership, their conferences and themes, and all of their contact information. It's invaluable if you want to speak in front of the industry leaders in your fields (*every* industry and profession has multiple professional associations). Go here: https://www.associationexecs.com/national-trade-and-professional-associations-directory.

- *Speakers bureaus.* Speakers bureaus generally represent speakers for hire to global organizations. Some are literally run by one person out of a spare room, but others are huge operations. They charge 25–30 percent of the gross fee. Some bureaus are terrific; some are horrid. As a new speaker, the best way to be represented is through an introduction from an existing client. However, like bank loans, when you really need them, you can't get them, and when you no longer need them, everyone wants to offer them. My advice is to eschew bureaus as you get started, unless one comes to you with an offer. *And never pay a bureau to be in their catalog, critique a video, or anything else.* Those practices are intended merely to make money from speakers, not help them make money.

This section isn't intended to give you specific speaking techniques or stage devices.[4] However, here are the most effective ways to gain *business* through your speaking efforts, whether paid or unpaid:

Alanism
Speak in front of nonbuyers to hone your skills and get comfortable. But then migrate to speaking only to buyers to hone your business and get wealthy.

- Come early and stay late. Network and socialize with the audience and the company executives before your session and after it. Stay an extra day if you can and it makes sense.

- If there is a bigger-name speaker on the agenda, meet that speaker, share some conversation, and when you are on stage say, "I was speaking with Joan, whom you heard this morning (or whom you'll hear tomorrow), and we agreed that...." This will enhance your credibility.

- Use "parachute stories," which are stories you drop into the speech to prove your points but also shine favorably on you. For example, if you wanted to make a case about motivation being intrinsic, say, "I was working on a motivational dilemma at a major financial institution and we found that if we changed...."

- Record your presentations if allowed, preferably on video. The host organization will sometimes be doing this anyway. If not, see if you can arrange for it (always use two cameras, one on you and one on the audience). If you work with the speaker's bureaus mentioned above, they will require a demo video of your work as a quality-control check. Even informally, this is a good idea. When I spoke at Harvard, they asked if they could make an informal recording and give me a copy for my own use. It's one of the most popular on my website today.

To summarize: start speaking in simple and unpressured situations, build your confidence and exposure, then move to opportunities with buyers. If you're paid, fine; if you're not, still fine.

Wholesale and Retail

When I say *wholesale*, I mean "corporate." This is where (almost always) a single buyer makes a decision to purchase your value for his or her operation, department, responsibilities, and so forth. When I say *retail*, I mean an individual purchase. Even though the purchaser may be paying out of a business account as a solo practitioner, nevertheless, you're making that sale to people purchasing for themselves.

Some aspects of consulting focus solely on the corporate market: organization development, change management, organizational redesign, M&As, and so forth.

Some aspects focus solely on retail, such as self-improvement, career development, and life balance.

Some aspects can focus on both, such as coaching, planning, innovation, and problem solving.

In the middle we have *SMEs* (small- to medium-sized enterprises), where an owner has between a few and hundreds of employees, and revenues of anywhere from $1 million to $200 million. (Definitions about size vary.) These business owners (if in the consulting profession, these would be boutique consulting firms) are interested in both personal fulfillment (quality of life, discretionary time, legacy) and business advancement (market share, valuation, margins). This, too, is a huge market.

Whether you specialize or not is up to you. I've discussed earlier the benefit of having large numbers of true buyers. But here are some guidelines and traits that may help you to understand the advantages and disadvantages of each market:

Corporate Benefits

- Larger average projects
- Multiple buyers in any one organization
- Prestigious names that carry weight with prospects
- Can be approached through major trade associations
- Multiple sites and often global
- Strong possibilities for repeat business
- Strong referral sources
- Rational decision making

Corporate Disadvantages

- Hard-to-reach buyers who are often shielded
- Often prefer larger consulting firms

- Will sometimes defer to procurement
- Will sometimes defer to human resources
- Large political and turf issues in many cases
- Legal departments often approve contracts
- Sometimes payment rules draconian (e.g., 120 days)[5]

SME Benefits

- Easy to locate buyer (owner)
- Smaller, controllable projects
- Fast responses/decisions
- Can see immediate improvement
- Strong peer-to-peer reference

SME Disadvantages

- Highly emotional decisions[6]
- Tend to be very price sensitive, not ROI driven
- Can be quite demanding, for example, require your presence often
- Accustomed to having their own way, not taking suggestions
- Family involvement in the business

Retail Benefits

- Single, obvious buyer
- Quick decisions
- Brief projects/coaching
- Huge numbers
- High evangelization probabilities
- Social media highly effective
- Often leads to/involves passive income (see following section)

Retail Disadvantages

- Relatively low fee
- Usually high competition
- At low end, very price sensitive
- Demands credit card acceptance and secure "store" on your site
- Theft of IP
- Can be disproportionately demanding

Alanism

I've worked in wholesale and retail, and while wholesale provides large fees, I've found the volume of retail potential far more attractive and have found there are ways to combine high fees with retail sales.

Thus, when you're selling in the SME marketplace to business owners, you're often making a retail sale (single person) in a wholesale environment (small business). Don't get hung up on that. Just be aware that the smaller the business, the more emotional the buying decision, and the larger the business, the more rational the buying decision.

No buyer in JPMorgan Chase or Boeing or Prudential is going to debate whether to invest money with you or use it for a new home! However, that buyer might be wondering whether the project you're proposing to improve the department's performance will also improve his or her reputation and chances for advancement!

Alanism

Logic makes people think; emotion makes them act. All sales have a strong emotional factor, professional and personal, to which you must appeal.

If you look back to the accelerant curve, you'll see that many of your value offerings—for example, coaching, workshops (on a public basis for individuals and/or in-house for larger firms), and skills building—are relevant to all the groups above.

Now let's look at how to make money while you sleep.

Passive Income

Passive income is generally a vault item on the accelerant curve. It consists of people purchasing products or services from you with no immediate, active participation on your part.

Examples of pure passive income would include:

- Books, booklets, ebooks
- Subscriptions
- Manuals and lists
- Access to downloads
- Access to past recordings (audio and video)

Note also that such passive income draws people to your site and other services, which also makes it an attractor (left side of the accelerant curve), even though you may be making quite a bit of money.

Normally, passive income is most attainable when you have a strong brand. On my site, alanweiss.com, you'll find a wide variety of passive income alternatives. As just one specific example, go here: https://www.alanweiss.com/store/growth-access/allaccess-program.

I've compiled here a huge amount of my prior body of work: text, workshops, audio, video, interviews, electronic offerings, and so forth. For one fee, someone can buy lifetime access. I add to it quarterly. So people are paying a fee to access this work, which requires zero additional time on my part since it's all been created for other uses and stored here.

Obviously, the longer you're in business and the stronger your brand, the easier it is. However, as long as we're talking about becoming a marketer, you should be thinking about it. What about taking all your blog posts (or newsletters) after a year and instead of archiving them for free putting them into a document that can be purchased on your site? What if you took every illustration and graphic you've created over the past year and put it into book form on your site?[7]

As you move forward and begin to fill your accelerant curve and develop work for your business that remains your property, consider its potential to be repurposed as passive income.

If you do sell things from your site, you'll need a merchant account. You can set up Mastercard, Visa, and Diners Club acceptance with your bank if it's a major institution, and directly with American Express. You'll be required to abide by privacy laws and Internet protective measures, which is very positive. Your specific pages will read https instead of http, meaning they are secure. Go to www.alanweiss.com and you'll see my certifications at the bottom.

Another definition I use for passive income is that it's close to home. In other words, I've built a retreat center in my home, and I also have a relationship with properties within 30 minutes of my home. I consider these workshops and retreats to be passive income because I sleep in my own bed and am merely commuting. You may not agree with that definition, which is fine, but for me it encompasses almost all of my coaching work—which is considerable—that I conduct by phone, Skype, and Zoom.

Although I'm interactive with people, not leaving my home at all is passive income to me.

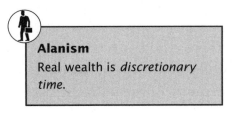

Alanism
Real wealth is *discretionary time.*

Passive income, no matter how you choose to define it, is the key to discretionary time, since it produces revenues either with no work (product purchases), low work (phone coaching), or close work (in your home or neighborhood). If you look on nearly any best-selling business book author's site, you'll find passive income galore.

Chapter 3 Definitions

Wholesale: A corporate purchase made by a single buyer covering groups of people, with the check usually produced by an accounts payable or procurement function.

Retail: An individual purchase for personal use by an individual (even if a solo practitioner with a business entity), with the check usually created by that person.

SME: A small- to medium-sized business (enterprise), the parameters of which vary depending on what source you're using, but generally businesses with more than a dozen employees and perhaps hundreds, and revenues of from $1 million to $200 million. It's a broad range.

Passive income: Income derived from no, low, or local labor, based on IP you've previously generated for this purpose or other purposes and recycled.

Discretionary time: Time completely under your control when you can choose to work, play, or both without any influence from others.

Notes

1. These are coaching methodologies. See my book *Million Dollar Coaching* for an in-depth description (McGraw-Hill, 2011).

2. For example, a local real estate office of 20 people that belongs to a billion-dollar parent.

3. Introduce yourself to the executive director and indicate you're available if a conference coming to town needs a local speaker to reduce travel expenses, or needs a replacement for a speaker who had to cancel at the last minute.

4. See my book *Million Dollar Speaking* (McGraw-Hill, 2011).

5. Companies such as Cisco take four months by policy to pay small businesses and solo practitioners, which I find reprehensible and unethical. Unfortunately, it's not illegal.

6. For example, should I spend money on the business or put it into my kids' college fund?

7. Which is exactly what I did in self-publishing *The Great Big Book of Process Visuals* (Las Brisas Research Press, 2000) and *The SECOND Great Big Book of Process Visuals* (Las Brisas Research Press, 2007), which are available on my site and on Amazon.com.

Technology for the Next Nine Seconds

A woman wrote me quite indignantly after I wrote a book called *The Million Dollar Consulting™ Toolkit* (John Wiley & Sons, 2006), which she had read it about six months later. She castigated me for not including the latest developments in technology. I asked her if I should visit everyone who purchased the book and insert new pages every month or so. She indignantly wrote a nasty review on Amazon.com!

Thus, take what follows as my attempt to align you with productive and supportive technology, knowing full well that you may be supersonically transported around the world by the time this is published!

The Greatest Technology Myths

In consulting, technology is an augmentation, not the solution. Our job is to *improve the client's condition through our expertise and advice*. It is not to do so by doing the client's work. That is what coders do and other technology subcontractors do who often call themselves consultants. But they're not; they're simply temporary employees.

Alanism
A contractor provides a
pair of hands. A consultant
provides a brain.

Technology is changing hourly. I currently see holographic images give me directions in airports. We can take part in virtual meetings and delegate work to virtual assistants. Yet we still hear lame excuses such as, "I'll be out of town, so I can't make a decision or get back to you until I return." I guess that person doesn't own a cell phone and can't use a computer!

I found to my surprise the other day that a call to my cell also appears and can be answered on my iPad, laptop, and desktop computer.

I'll try to focus on *technology processes* here, sensitive to the fact that technology content changes every nine seconds. And I thought I'd begin with the most blatant myths about technology so that you can avoid them, and then move on to what does make sense as you begin this journey.

Myth #1: SEO Matters

SEO stands for "search engine optimization," and its intent is to raise your profile on Internet search engines through a variety of techniques so that your name comes up more frequently and people can find you more easily. The problem here is twofold:

1. Your ideal buyers do not use such indicators and are usually not involved with what such techniques produce. SEO does not rate inclusion on the marketing gravity chart (Figure 2.1) displayed earlier.
2. Everyone and their dog does this, so the noise is deafening, and no one really stands out.

This is the concept for which we receive thousands of spam emails from people working out of their bedrooms to people working all over the globe promising riches for your small investment. You're better off shouting on a rooftop. (Soon, SEO will be replaced with another lame technique, and it will make no difference.)

Here's what I received in an email, addresses removed, as I was writing this segment, with no editing:

"I am a Business Consultant specializing in helping businesses start up and grow. We offer highly skilled and experienced developers in fields such as PHP Development, E-Commerce, and SEO service.

"Our full service design firm offers the following services and products:

"1. Website Designing/Development (WordPress, Magneto, E-commerce, CodeIgniter, Joomla, OsCommerce, PHP Development, Shopify, PrestaShop, OpenCart Development, and SEO service)

"2. E-Commerce Solutions, any type of website Development. Mobile iPhone, Android Apps Development.

"If you are looking for a new website or any kind of upgrades in your current website then please feel free to share your requirement."

Right.

Myth #2: Your Website Is a Sales Platform

At best, your website is a credibility statement. It may be sought out for background and validity once someone is interested in you. But true buyers do not troll the web looking at websites.

You, personally, may buy a chair or a computer or a phone from the web. But you're not going to buy a car, and you're certainly not going to choose a physician or an attorney (at least, I hope not). You're going to ask friends—peers—for their recommendations. After receiving those recommendations, you may go to the recommended person's site. Fair enough.

Don't let anyone tell you to improve your site or build an expensive one because the additional business will pay for it. Sites are obsolete almost as soon as they're completed because of the frantic pace of technology. After 30 years in this business, my people are just completing only my fourth site overhaul. I don't need the latest technology, just reliable technology. And don't forget, I'm in the retail business and use my site to sell products and services, so it's far more of a sales mechanism than yours will probably ever need to be.

Myth #3: Social Media Platforms Are Important for Marketing

Facebook is primarily a social gathering space. The noise about politics, health issues, travel, conspiracy theories, and cooking is deafening. Using Facebook for marketing is like writing on a wall and expecting people to pay attention. It's primarily an ego vehicle.

LinkedIn has some promise, in that you can form private groups around topics. There are instances where you're found directly or via a third party based on something you've published or your profile. But the overwhelming activity on LinkedIn is about people looking for work and thinking anyone who's linked is a prospective employer or referrals source.

Twitter is useful for you to practice publishing value within a tight character limit (though that challenge is lessened since they expanded the limit). If you use it for that purpose a few times a week, it's a good exercise and quick to do.

YouTube is another wasteland that has some intelligent promotional videos, but they're intertwined with pornography, pet tricks, and juvenile exchanges.

Once popular Klout.com is long closed. Its purpose was to tell you how "popular" you are by combining interest paid to you on these platforms. But the numbers of followers on any of them is irrelevant if they're not your buyers or at least recommenders, and they very seldom are. You can't pay the mortgage with numbers of links, followers, or friends.

Myth #4: The Generational Differences Affect Technology and Marketing

Have you seen grandmothers and grandfathers industrially punching keyboards on iPads, smartphones, and other tablets? I certainly have.

You can hardly be a top executive or a business owner today without being technologically savvy. They may not know how to edit movies or use Instagram or make PDF files. But they can certainly use email, websites, electronic newsletters, blogs, and so on. They can receive and sign proposals electronically.

And younger executives are not going to eschew email and traditional means of communication for every new Pinterest that comes along. They're going to use what *most* of their employees can use and *all* of their customers can use.

Myth #5: You Should Always Adopt the Latest Technology

Only use what works for you. I've estimated that on my desktop computer, laptop computer, iPhone, and iPad I use about 20 percent of the available firepower. But I use that 20 percent to about 98 percent effectiveness.

In other words, use what works optimally and don't try to force new technologies into your procedures unless they prove to work optimally for you. You should probably update your software whenever new versions are released, but even then you want to make sure the improvements are relevant and useful for you.

The Role of a Website Might Surprise You

Let's examine one of the crucial myths above in more detail. Your website is a credibility statement, not a sales tool, especially in wholesale markets. So, what should be included, and how should it look?

First, don't attempt creating a site yourself, even if you're adept in technology. You wouldn't accept (I hope) a prospect's telling you that they can do it themselves instead of hiring you for your expertise. Never try to save money with less than professional work.

Second, find someone good through references from people you trust who were in your position (starting out) not long ago and who have websites you admire. (Throughout this book, we're talking about the great power of peer-to-peer references in the sales process.) Don't choose:

- Someone from an Internet list selling services
- Someone from a foreign country whom you can't verify
- Someone doing it part-time to make a few bucks
- Someone who primarily works for large companies

Does that leave anyone?! Yes, ask around and you'll find there are professionals who do this, charge by the hour, and can create a perfectly suitable website. These sites are fungible, in that they can be changed on an ongoing basis at any time, and even thrown out and replaced. (In fact, as you prosper and grow, they should be, because you'll have even more credibility to express.)

Ask for references and examples from the person tentatively selected, call the references and ask the best and worst about working with them (if there is no "worst" move on; someone's lying), and look at others' sites they've done. Once you're made the choice, give them a budget (so many hours at an agreed rate) with metrics for approval (see below) and after a deposit of about 20 percent pay nothing else until the metrics are being met and pay the final balance only at the end when you are satisfied.

Alanism

Web designers are chronically late. This is the buyer's fault. Pay the preponderance of the fee at the conclusion, and if the designer falls behind on the way, demand they make better progress or fire them. Most of all, choose someone who has worked well for others you respect.

Once you have the proper resource, here's what you basically need:

Home page. This is where most people will initially go, and what you will put in your signature file and collateral—for example, alanweiss.com. On your home page you should have:

- Your photo, preferably "environmental," meaning not just a head shot but rather you with clients in a group or at a client site. Always use a professional photographer. If you are doing close-ups or head shots, have someone there who can help with hair, makeup, lighting, and so on.

- Typical client results. These don't have to be *actual* client results, which you might not yet have if you're very new to the profession. Rather, typically what results can your clients expect? These should be *business outcomes* and might include, for example:
  - Faster commercialization of products
  - Reduced closing time at less cost
  - Reduced attrition
  - Higher margins
  - More referral business from customers

- Your value proposition.

- A few testimonials, which rotate. Ideally, these should be on video (of 30 to 60 seconds), which can be taken on a smartphone. But text would work at the outset. They should rotate on the page, with enough time to watch or read each one before moving on. If you don't have project testimonials at this point, use character testimonials from people who know you. Replace them as you can—as mentioned, the site is always changeable.

That's it for now. Consider this home page as real estate and use it wisely, as you would actual real estate: the grounds are attractive, not overgrown or crowded, colorful, and professionally maintained.

Inside, meaning pages that can be accessed from the home page via menu selections, you should have (as you progress):

- *ALL of your contact information.* Include a physical address. Some consultants don't do this in an electronic age, but a client can't send you a physical check or a package electronically. Include your email and phone as well and how to follow you on Twitter, LinkedIn, and so forth as appropriate.

- *Case studies as you develop them.* These should be one paragraph in this fashion:
  - *Situation.* A financial firm was seeking to cross-sell its leading products to build revenues.
  - *Intervention.* We interviewed existing customers, prospects, and retail store managers to devise a better system for cross-selling, and then trained them and their direct managers.
  - *Resolution.* Cross-selling improved in the ensuing six months by 18 percent, for an annualized improvement of $3.4 million.

  You should have two or three of these as you develop them for your various areas of expertise.

- *A client list.* Never say "partial client list" and provide four names, because everyone knows they're your only four clients! Wait until you have 20 or more. (If you're ever asked, point-blank, with whom you work, simply say, "My clients' names, of course, are confidential, as yours would be if we work together.)

- *Position papers, or white papers.* These are two to five pages of your beliefs (position) on various topics related to your work. Make them edgy and provocative. Example: "Four reason why you're holding too many meetings, wasting too much time, and what to do about it." Include photos, graphics, and so forth as you see fit, and put your copyright and contact information on every one (they are sometimes downloaded and shared). You can also place articles here you publish elsewhere, including social media.

That's about it. *Very few people are going to read the inside pages of your site.* That's not a commentary on you or your quality, just the reality of today's attention spans. Thus, make sure your home page is highly effective, because that's where most people start and stop.

Here are some examples of good websites at this writing to give you an idea and to reify what we've discussed above:

- Lisalarter.com
- Engageselling.com
- Stevengaffney.com
- Bates-communications.com

Social Media Platforms Are Often Tilted

You'll note first that these are not called "business media platforms." That's because these platforms are a gallimaufry of opinions, conspiracy theories, health suggestions, medical advice, vacation photos, soft pornography, and, occasionally, business ideas of merit.

So the platform is often skewed to the non-serious or even ridiculous. And the noise level is quite high, meaning you're drowned in a cacophony of warnings, recommendations, and ego. On any given day you can find a LinkedIn article with a title something like "Six Reasons to Never Hold a Meeting" followed by another with the title "Six Reasons to Hold More Meetings."

There is no barrier to entry on social media. I'm writing this on the Jersey Shore, and at the beginning of the amusements on the boardwalk is that same psychic I mentioned earlier who's been here for over a decade. She had to face more licensing and certifications than anyone choosing to join a social media platform.

Worse, there is a crazed egalitarianism that arises. A man on LinkedIn wrote me for free consulting advice. I told him I don't coach for free (I generally accept anyone who wants to link, befriend, or follow—more on that below). He told me that since we're peers I was obligated to do so. I asked him if he and the Dalai Lama subscribed to the same newspapers, would they be peers?

So, why do I raise the issue, and why am I on social media? For the following nine reasons, which also pertain to you:

1. We need to build a body of work. By publishing on LinkedIn and Twitter especially (Facebook is overwhelmingly social in my opinion), we do create the opportunity to distribute intellectual property on a frequent basis.

2. We never really know where our next "hit" is coming from. Since these platforms are essentially cost free for article placement (though not for some forms of promotion and boosts), they are very appropriate for people new to the profession.

3. People who do read our material and find it useful will tend to spread the word. There is a chain reaction that takes place—"viral" is the stereotypical term—which can propel us into new audiences.

4. It's not vital to talk *solely* to buyers. There are recommenders on social media who can introduce us to others.

5. On LinkedIn you can form private groups that constitute a nascent community of prospects. You can pump value into these groups on a frequent basis, even develop your own frequently asked questions, and, once successful, you can include buyers for evangelization purposes.

6. All of these platforms allow for multimedia so that you can enhance your messages with photos, graphs, artwork, audio, and video. You can provide links to your site, blog, and other destinations.

7. We can repurpose our materials and use them in slightly varied forms (or even the same forms) on multiple platforms.

8. We can create "series" (for example, #7 in the 20 top ways to reduce turnover) that people begin to follow and so become drawn into your orbit. (This is all on the left side of the accelerant curve in Figure 3.1)

9. We can, if we use our time prudently, follow, befriend, and link with a few people who can keep us apprised of the state of the art and indeed provide free learning.[1]

There are two very important bottom line aspects to social media usage that are interrelated.

First, these and other platforms (for example, YouTube) can be huge time dumps. You can find yourself prepared to spend a few minutes browsing, and before you know it, two hours have elapsed. An analogy: I use my iPhoto album as a screen saver, and sometimes my wife will watch the family photos and stand there for 30 minutes. I had to put a 10-minute limit on the screen saver photos so that the screen went black after that time. That would break her out of her reverie, but there's no such fail-safe for Facebook, for example. You need the discipline to limit your exposure. I allot about 10 minutes in the morning to post on social media, and that's it. I seldom visit for the rest of the day, and if I do, it's brief.

Second, in order to reduce the likelihood of spending far more time than the ROI provides, if you want to more heavily engage in social media, use a professional. There are experts in social media marketing who simply want to take your money and plaster some of your stuff on the virtual walls. But there are others who can intelligently take excerpts from your work and ensure that you're represented frequently every week with the kinds of messages you want to send to prospects. They will help you create that body of work. You can probably secure such services for somewhere between $500 and $1,500 a month, depending on frequency and other needs.

> **Alanism**
> There's a reason we call them "courts of law" and not "courts of justice," and there's a reason they're called "social" media and not "business" media.

Finally, I want to mention blogging here. Though not technically a social media platform, blogging is inexpensive (you merely need someone to set up the blog, probably the same person who set up your website, and have the discipline to post several times a week).

Blog posts can be a sentence, a paragraph, or a lengthier piece. You can include visuals. My blog (contrarianconsulting.com) has guest articles, my articles in various categories (for example, marketing, ethics), cartoons, podcasts, videos, and so forth. The key here is frequency. People will use *RSS* (Really Simple Syndication) to be informed every time you post, which is a great way to build attention. But this will only happen with frequent, diverse, high-value postings. You can use your social media resource noted above to also populate your blog site if you so desire.

Social media are far less important than peer-to-peer reference, and most of the latter does *not* occur on social media but rather in person and by other means.[2] It doesn't hurt to be there and may give you some advantage if you're prudent in your use and reasonable in your expectations.

Remaining Cutting Edge without Hurting Yourself

If you strive to have the latest technology with state-of-the-art applications and mastery of your software with multiple backups and smart devices, you can do this. But only if that's what you do all day long and aren't trying to engage in the consulting business.

However, assuming you're reading this fine book because you want to be a professional consultant (and, eventually, an expert, thought leader, and icon), you need to temper your urge to possess the newest and the best. You're probably driving a car that's more than a few months old, watching stuff on television that you recorded from some time ago or is a repeat, and dining at longtime favorite restaurants.

So why do you need the latest geegaws and space-age technology to go about your business?

Someone asked me recently why I wore an expensive watch when a smartphone has the time on it. I told him that, first, you don't want to pull out your phone in front of a client when you're curious about the time (or determining if you're on schedule while making a speech). And second, a watch today is an accessory, like a ring or a woman's earrings or necklace. Just because a phone has the time on it doesn't mean it should be the default method for determining what time it is.

This is a relationship business. It's not a technology business. Technology can augment what you do, but we're not in business to augment technology. And, ironically, in a technological age, we shouldn't accept antediluvian, pretechnology excuses, such as, "I'm away on business, so I can't respond to your proposal." Really? You don't use a computer or a mobile device?

Here's some advice to keep your time oriented toward the business at hand—attracting, converting, and expanding client business—using technology intelligently and inexpensively.

You Don't Need Infinite Backups

When I worked at Prudential Insurance in the late 1960s and early 1970s, a triplicate copy of all of our work in Group Insurance Administration went to the Scranton Files. Being a young kid and tasked with the job of streamlining and reducing costs, I wrote to the Scranton Files to find out what they did with the triplicate copy—and received no answer.

I went around to some old-timers and found that the Scranton Files were actually abandoned coal mines outside of Scranton, Pennsylvania, and the idea in the 1950s was that the company would store records there deep underground as a safeguard against atom bombs. In other words, after the holocaust, we would come to the surface and continue selling insurance!!

The idea had been abandoned by more intelligent management, but not the procedure. So I abandoned it with no consequence except saving time and money.

You need a good backup for your records. You can use all kinds of options in the cloud, or external drives, or both. But that's it. You don't need quintuple backups to protect your records in the event another piece of space junk slams into the Yucatán once again and we all go the way of the tyrannosaurs. Keep it simple and make your backup automated. You may want to check for better or safer alternatives once a year.

Don't Use Email as a Storage System, and Reduce Your Email in General

This is a chronic problem. I've seen systems with thousands of emails piled up and no priorities or signs of intelligent thought.

Create electronic files and stow only highly relevant email in them. Do not think for a moment you need the equivalent of the Library of Congress to capture every email you've ever sent or received.

Typical Files

- Clients by name
- Prospects by name
- Non-client projects by name (for example, writing a book)
- Articles and publishing by name
- Financial (revenues, invoices, and so forth)
- Personal (vacation plans, investments)
- Graphics and illustrations, including photos for business

Typical Things to Keep

- Contracts and proposals
- Published materials
- Client correspondence that is important for current projects
- Templates and samples
- Research or ideas for publishing or services
- Hotel and travel information and itineraries

Amend this as you see fit, but *do not* automatically keep every email you send or receive. Also, send far fewer. It's easy to hit a key and say "thanks," but it's not always necessary, nor is "you're welcome" or "nice talking to you" or "how's the weather?" If you were still sending out hard copy letters, you certainly wouldn't be wasting time with all these trivialities, and you shouldn't now, either.

Use the Appropriate Communication Vehicle

At this writing, Zoom is the best vehicle for two-person or multiperson meetings. Skype is much less reliable. There are other fine options, such as GoToMeeting™, and there will be more by the time you're reading this.

Choose something appropriate for your needs. If it's just two of you, a phone may be better than all the razzle-dazzle. If you're going to conduct a webinar, then you'll need something appropriate for visuals and questions and answers. You don't need *the* best; you need *the best for your purposes.*

I want to make sure you're aware of the proper major communication sequence priorities:

1. In person
2. Zoom or equivalent
3. Phone
4. Email

If you can meet with a buyer or recommender (or media resource), do so. If you can't, talk by Zoom or something like it. If you can't do that, pick up the phone. *Only as a last resort, for important communications, use email.*

Why? Because email is easily discarded (advertently or inadvertently), is highly impersonal, is relatively easily stolen or hacked, and is of very low influence (being a communication among hundreds each day). I fall down laughing when I see email marked "urgent!" If it's "urgent," why don't you call?!

Just as you should stop obsessing about involvement with social media platforms, you should stop obsessing about your hardware, software, and peripheral equipment. I can understand better quality speakers, but I can't understand better photo editing software if you don't

Alanism
This is a relationship business. Technology may augment relationships but never replaces them and can sometimes just get in the way.

edit photos. I can understand a wireless keyboard, but not dictation software when you don't ever dictate (or where transcription software simply causes you more work).

And I can never understand a consultant who spends the predominant amount of precious time with technology instead of with buyers.

Using Social Media Selectively

Here's the latest wisdom from Lisa Larter, who is THE expert in Internet marketing for professional services (https://lisalarter.com):

When you venture into the world of consulting, most of the advice you hear will encourage you to be everywhere on social media.

Don't listen to it. If you spread yourself too thin, you'll struggle to generate any quality leads. While it's essential to establish credibility and create an effective social media network, there are some clear guidelines you need to consider in the process.

Choosing the Channel

Determine the best channel for you to connect and engage with your buyers. That means you need to put some time and effort in to uncover where your specific buyers hang out on social media. Invest some time up front in getting to know who your ideal buyer is and then go look at a handful of social media channels to identify the best one for you.

It doesn't make sense to spend all your time on Facebook if your buyers are to be found on LinkedIn.

Add Value and Build Your Credibility

Once you choose your channel, you need to identify the best way to demonstrate your expertise by sharing valuable content and IP. As well as sharing valuable content, it's vital to use the formats that make the most sense for the channels you've selected.

For example, LinkedIn is a powerful social channel for most consultants and offers two key ways for you to add value to your potential buyers: upload native videos that have been shot with your ideal buyer in mind and publish articles on LinkedIn Pulse.

If you want to add real value and continue to build credibility, you will need to share content on your channel of choice regularly, accompanied by an up-to-date bio, a description of your services, and a link to a modern and functioning website.

Build a Network and Be Responsive

Build your network slowly and gradually. Your network is of little use to you for business development if your connections consist solely of people you've never met in person. Make a habit of sending connection requests to people you know, people you've done business with, and people you've met in person at events.

If you do this on a regular basis, your network will become valuable to you, provided you are responsive. Social media is like voicemail and email; if someone sends you a message or comments on the content that you share, you need to respond quickly and demonstrate that you're more interested in building relationships than you are transactions.

In addition to being responsive, be proactive. Social media allows you to learn about the challenges and wins that your buyers and potential buyers experience every day. Pay attention to these details and interact with people regularly if you want to stay top of mind. The best time to ask for a referral is not five minutes after you've connected with someone you haven't spoken to in five years. Invest time in building solid, reliable relationships with your social network.

Use the Tools

Every social network offers you a suite of tools and reporting that can help you to measure how you are doing. Use these tools on a regular basis to track your progress and install useful tools such as the LinkedIn Insight Tag or Facebook Pixel on your website. In that way you can re-market to people who visit your site.

A word of warning: Don't get caught up in vanity metrics but pay attention to details that are important to you, such as the fact that your potential buyer is viewing your profile on a weekly basis on LinkedIn. It provides you with a perfect reason for checking in with them.

Social media can be a complete waste of time unless you choose the channel where your buyers hang out, and invest time in creating valuable content and in building stronger relationships with your network.

The data don't lie. Billions of people use social media via their mobile devices, multiple times each day. There is a very good chance your buyers are included in those numbers, and you want them to be able to find and connect with you in the very place where they are spending their time.

Thank you, Lisa!

Chapter 4 Definitions

SEO: Search engine optimization, meant to make you and your work easier to find on the Internet, but grossly overrated and hawked by technical people usually from overseas trying to make a buck.

RSS: Really Simple Syndication, enabling someone to be notified every time you post on your blog. This creates repeat visitors.

Notes

1. Join me on Twitter (http://twitter.com/BentleyGTCSpeed), Facebook (https://www.facebook.com/RockStarofConsulting), and LinkedIn (https://www.linkedin.com/in/alanweissphd).

2. Research conducted by Jonah Berger in *Contagious* (Simon & Schuster, 2016) and *Invisible Influence* (Simon & Schuster, 2017).

Chapter

Finding the Economic Buyer

We've covered the basics regarding mindset and support, logistics and legal, administrative and financial. These structures and relationships are important in your stability to generate *and sustain* business.

So now let's talk about how to obtain business, because you can't pay the mortgage or the rent with administrative support or positive vibes.

Saint Paul Was the First Virtual Marketer

Historically, we'd know very little about the advent of Christianity without Paul (originally Saul of Tarsus), who wrote extensively about the people and times of the person known as Jesus. Of the 27 New Testament books, 13 are attributed to Paul, and approximately half of Acts of the Apostles deals with Paul's life and works. Thus, about half of the New Testament stems from Paul and the people whom he influenced after his conversion on the road to Damascus.

I raise his exploits because he would travel, mostly by foot, to the Corinthians, Romans, Hebrews, Colossians, and so forth, and preach.

And in so doing he would tell them to go to preach to others, and so on. Without anything resembling technology, he was able to spread the word. And, in fact, within 300 years of the death of Jesus, what we now call Christianity had grown from a dozen followers to 60 million within the Roman Empire. This growth was exponential, far more than could be expected from normal communications and conversions.[1]

That incredible growth was an example of early viral marketing. The more you attempt to spread the word *using people and devices most likely to spread the word farther*, the more people will learn of your talents and brand, your value and ability to help.

So the question becomes, in terms of those people and devices, *whom do we want to receive the message?*

We spoke earlier in terms of our ideal buyer. Our ideal buyer is the economic buyer—that person who can authorize payment (or actually write the check) for our products and services (our value). In retail, it's the individual customer. In SMEs, it's usually the owner or president. In wholesale, there can be scores of economic buyers within one Fortune 1000 company. They will either have *P&L* (profit and loss) responsibility or will head large support departments, such as finance or operations.

HR Stands for "Hardly Relevant"

Alanism
Use noneconomic buyers only to reach an economic buyer; otherwise, you're wasting your time on people who can't say "yes" but can say "no."

Very few lessons in this book are as important as this one: you are wasting your time if you enter into discussions with and become peers of noneconomic buyers. Once an executive sees you as a peer of subordinates, you will never be considered a peer of executives. And as for the other reasons:

- No internal person will ever represent you with the passion and commitment that you will for yourself. They are too worried about pleasing their superiors and not making waves.

- Lower-level people are overwhelmingly concerned about deliverables and implementation schemes, and not about results and outcomes. Yet the ROI for projects is in the outcome, not the task.

- Nonbuyers want the bureaucracy satisfied, forms filled out, placement on approved vendor lists, and so on.

- They have no real budgets of their own, can't move money or reallocate it, and cannot take on unplanned investments.

- In general, they are not seen as credible or as peers by their own line clients, who basically ask them to do busy work (e.g., find job candidates) but not essential work (e.g., organization restructuring or strategy formulation).

Almost universally, people in human resources, learning and development, and related functions in the organization are not buyers and never will be. I stress this here because they *are*, often, easy to see and will meet with you until the cows come home. But you don't get paid for meetings, and these meetings never end. This is the La Brea Tar Pits of organizations. You can disappear in there and never be heard from again within that company.

I have a standing bet of $1,000 with some of my colleagues that they can't come up with three HR executives (not people who rotate in and out, but lifelong HR people) who have become the CEO (chief executive officer) of a Fortune 1000 company over the past five years. There have been people named as CEO who were executive and senior vice presidents of many functions—actuaries, sales executives, general counsels, chief financial officers—but none from HR. Why? Because these are not highly respected functions in most organizations, and the people who head them are not regarded within the organization as top people.

Now, that all may sound harsh, but I'm here for you, not them. And I want you to know that HR is not a springboard or an assist but, rather, quicksand.

Thus, your job is to find and meet with your ideal economic buyers (meaning the economic buyers in your marketplace). If and when you encounter lower-level people by means of referral or happenstance, you can elevate your connection with this kind of language:

- *The way I work is to meet with the person making the decision for, and funding, the project. Would you be kind enough to introduce me?*

- *Who owns the budget for this project? That's the person I need to meet.*

- *Ethically, I must meet the person with the fiduciary responsibility for the launch of the work.*

- *I must hear from the lips of the buyer what his or her expectations are so that I can assess whether they can be reasonably accomplished.*

- *I need to meet the person making the investment so that we can both determine whether we're right for each other for this type of partnership.*

I think you can see the direction. If you sometimes hear in response:

- *I've been tasked with finding resources for this work, and it's my decision who will be recommended.*

Then you say:

- *I appreciate that, but you're asking me questions that I can't answer (or asking me for a proposal that I can't provide) unless I speak with the owner of this project.*

And, in worst case:

- *If you can't or won't introduce me, I'll contact the project owner independently. Do you want me to mention our conversation or not?*

These are the words to employ, and this isn't language I developed over the years after I had developed a major brand and could become bold. This was language I developed early that enabled me to build my brand and become bold, *because you can't just waste your time trying to please people who are unwilling and unable to make a purchase from you.*

Like Paul, consider this your revelation on the road to Damascus, and as you begin your viral marketing to grow your own practice, make sure that it's with communities of buyers, not gatekeepers. Going viral isn't sufficient; in fact, it can be harmful, if not done with the right people.

Charging Past Gatekeepers

I'm going to refer to those who are nonbuyers as *gatekeepers*. Like any gatekeeper in history, their job, as they perceive it, is to prevent people from walking in without the proper credentials and without their approval, and certainly to prevent them from wandering around if they do get in.

I realize that this will sound draconian, but the only way in which these people can help you is by rapidly introducing you to people who, in fact, *can buy from you, can purchase your value.* The problem is that they are relatively easy to meet, enjoy taking all kinds of time talking about esoteric plans and abstruse methodologies, and are as big a time sink as YouTube, but without the entertainment value.

I'm taking the time to explain this in no uncertain terms, because this is a pivotal point in your early, later, and ultimate success: you cannot afford to spend time with such people, to be recognized as their peers, or to submit information (or, heaven forfend, proposals) to them.

How serious is this? I've been in the consulting business since I was 26, and have had my own solo practice since 1986. I have worked in all that time with exactly three—*tres, trois, drei, sān*—gatekeepers who were extremely helpful. These three people consistently introduced me to my ideal buyers in their Fortune 1000 firms because they saw their jobs as bringing the best resources against the most pressing organizational issues, and *not* as preserving their fiefdoms, gaining personal credit, or protecting their jobs. You may be thinking, "Fine, I'll look for them." Well, all three came to me, and those three are among thousands of gatekeepers I had to circumvent, debate, or simply barge through.

Low-level people—and as I've mentioned, in our profession they are usually from HR, learning and development, talent management, or some related euphemism—*are* the ones who troll the Internet, looking at various sites. They are the ones who have little interest or understanding of corporate results (for example, higher margins) but rather focus on task and methodology (for example, how many people in how many training programs, and what does the outline look like). They are basically people whom the organization doesn't deem fit to be in more important positions.

Digression

One of the unpleasant findings in consulting is that HR and other staff positions, such as administration, or legal, or accounting, or procurement, often have women and minorities leading them. These are fine people, but the organization is using them to prove it's diverse, counting them as executives, but not placing them in positions to head sales, manufacturing, marketing, R&D, and so forth. I consider that a corporate crime. We talk sometimes of glass ceilings, but I've found that there are actually glass walls.

You have limited time and energy, and your marketing thrust must be toward those people who are true economic buyers, who control budgets, and who can move money. Money and time are priorities, not resources. There is no such condition as "we don't have the money" or "we don't have the time" although lower-level people will consistently use these excuses, since they are, essentially, powerless.

Real buyers can move money and make time by taking them from other, less productive, less promising endeavors. It's up to us to prove that our value deserves priority treatment. But that argument can only be made with a true buyer, not a gatekeeper.

There are three ways to deal with a gatekeeper. After all, the gatekeeper might be the one who contacted you, or to whom you're introduced. They are starting points *if they are seen as departure points and springboards.*

Apply Rational Self-Interest

This should be your starting point. Before engaging in any detailed conversations, ask who owns the project, who controls the budget, who will evaluate it at the end of the day. Then suggest how the two of you should approach that person, with you providing the insights for improvement and the gatekeeper getting the credit for bringing you in and working to implement the project after approval.

This will work perhaps 15 percent of the time. Most gatekeepers are loath to bring anyone to their bosses or a line officer because they are fearful and insecure.

Apply Guile

If the first option fails, then say this: "Ethically, I must meet the person with the fiduciary responsibility for the project to ensure that the expectations are realistic and we believe we can work together to achieve them."

Often, "ethically" and "fiduciary" will sufficiently scare the gatekeeper into sending you upwards like a hand grenade about to explode. You can also add, "Frankly, I'd be surprised that your organization would work with any consultant who didn't demand that type of meeting at the outset."

This approach will work about 15 percent of the time.

Apply Force

If the first two don't work, you have nothing to lose with the remaining 70 percent, so you blow up the gatekeeper. Tell that person that since he or she refuses to make the introduction, and you now know who the actual buyer is, you will contact them directly. Then ask, "Should I mention this conversation or not?"

I know that sounds threatening, but you have absolutely nothing to lose because the gate is being kept closed. So you need to barge through it. We'll talk about how best to begin conversations with economic buyers later in the book, but you can't have that conversation until you're in their office, and you get can't to their office from outside the castle.

Here are some questions to ask to find the real economic buyer. Keep these in your briefcase or portfolio and by your phone until you're accustomed to asking at least some of them:

- Whose budget will support this initiative?
- Who can immediately approve this project?
- To whom will people look for support, approval, and credibility?
- Who controls the resources required to make this happen?
- Who has initiated this request?
- Who will claim responsibility for the results?
- Who will be seen as the main sponsor and/or champion?
- Do you have to seek anyone else's approval?
- Who will accept or reject proposals?
- If you and I were to shake hands, could I begin tomorrow?

Key point: The larger the organization, the more the number of economic buyers. They need not be the CEO or owner but must be able to authorize and produce payment. Committees are never *economic buyers. Someone controls the budget.*

To summarize: very few behaviors, early in your career, will serve you as well as the determination and forceful action to get through or around gatekeepers. You may well enlist their aide in moving upwards, but my track record isn't very good in that regard, yet my track record once I move past them is virtually unequalled.

The Peerage

The "peerage" means those holding an honorary or hereditary title, especially in the United Kingdom. I want to focus you on "peers," which means "equals."

In the following chapters we're going to walk into the buyer's office and close business. In the prior chapters we talked about mindset and

attitude. Those two condition meet when you actually find your ideal buyer and make contact.

Why is this so important? Because you're going to be talking to people with significant titles (or ownership), often in impressive offices, with secretaries and assistants, who make a lot of money, and who know their business quite well. That can be daunting when you stare out a window from 35 floors up or sit in an office larger than your first apart-

> **Alanism**
> You must see yourself as a peer of the buyer in terms of respective expertise and abilities and talents. If you see yourself as anything less, then you're just applying to be a part-time employee.

ment or watch a thousand people working under someone's auspices.

Sometimes you may ask yourself, "What on earth am I doing here? How can I possibly be of help?" (Try not to ask these questions out loud.)

You have to face these buyers as peers. After all, you are expert in your field of consulting and coaching. You bring intellectual property and new ideas. You are a breath of fresh air from outside the walls of the client establishment, where people are often woozy from breathing their own exhaust.

If you think I'm trying to build up your confidence, you're right! But let me depart from the dreaded motivational speech and provide some solid, pragmatic insights and practices.

Read

You must, first and foremost, achieve the peerage by being a businessperson. That means you need to read business publications and books as well as other sources. But here are the musts:

Read the *Wall Street Journal* every day. Subscribe to it in hard copy or online. Don't read every article, and you can forget about the cattle futures. But do look at the headlines and read those articles relevant for you—for example, on strategy, a particular industry or profession, finances, and so forth. I can obtain the *Journal* anywhere in the world (though sometimes a day late), and I never fail to read it. It also has a wonderful arts section and is probably the best-written newspaper in the country. (Outside of the United States you can also read it, or you may prefer *The Economist* or something similar.) Depending on your reading speed and comprehension, this should take 30–45 minutes.

Digression
I was making a speech in Missouri at a health-care organization, and was introduced at a reception to a board member who was the president of the largest trucking firm in the state. I recalled a *Journal* article from a couple of days prior reporting that Consolidated Freightways, a huge national shipper, had declared bankruptcy. I asked this man how that affected his own company, and he spoke for 30 minutes.

Also read your hometown newspaper daily (or the local paper if you're traveling). If you read about the arts, sports, and other issues as well, you'll be able to talk comfortably about a variety of topics. I've had many first-time contacts with buyers where I immediately asked, "Did you see the game last night?"

In Appendix B I've listed some books that I suggest you read to create a comprehensive knowledge of business in general and consulting in particular.

See

Look around you and try to understand what you see. Are you shopping in a store where you might wish to do business? Is the sales help initiating or aloof? Is the lighting appropriate? Is there a sufficient variety? Is signage clear?

In a bank, are the tellers polite? Do they know you by name? On an airline does the captain make an announcement greeting people? Is the boarding handled well?

When you meet a buyer, how does he or she dress: casually or more businesslike? What is the office like, a cubicle or a palace? Are there personal items and artwork? Are there pictures of family and pets? Does the buyer seem open to and interactive with employees?

I was once escorted around a huge office by a senior vice president and noticed that everyone stared. I thought this was not a good sign, and later asked his secretary, "Why do your people stare at a newcomer?" She replied, "Oh, they weren't staring at you, they were staring at my boss since he rarely leaves his office."

Hear

Listen for what's *really* being said. It's not what people tell you so much as it is what they don't choose to tell you! Are your questions answered casually and thoroughly, or is there some disingenuousness? What are people chatting about in the organization?

There have been plane crashes attributed to pilots' inattention to the controls while discussing changes in their retirement plans. I hear sales associates frequently talking about their exploits last night who can't tell you where certain products are because they don't use that time to learn their own business.

Are people responding to customers' and clients' honest requests, or are they reading scripts and trying to get them out of their way? Is there a positive buzz in the place or only a forlorn moan?

Feel

Finally, what's the vibe? Is your buyer upbeat and energetic or beaten down and cynical? Do you sense camaraderie or tyranny? I always feel a better vibe on Emirates airline than I do on United. I can walk into one American Airlines club and be greeted effusively but walk into another and barely be spoken to.

Is this a place in which you'd want to work? Are there people with whom you'd like to be colleagues? Is this a buyer with whom you'd like to partner?

I note these acts—read, see, hear, feel—as techniques you should use constantly until they become second nature. They will enable you to get the lay of the land and not be intimidated by buyers' surroundings when you enter them.

The key to believing you are a peer of the buyer and acting as one is to understand that we *all* have talents and problems, that we *all* face issues we need help resolving, and that healthy, positive people regard experts and their support as intelligent choices, signs of strength, not weakness.

You are about to partner with a buyer, not work for a buyer, or be delegated to others by that buyer. That's where you belong, and that's what success in this business is about.

The first sale is to yourself.

Chapter 5 Definitions

P&L: Profit and loss, which is often the metric upon which executives are evaluated for their units. People who have this accountability are usually buyers.

Gatekeeper: Anyone who perceives his or her job as protecting their boss and preventing others from reaching the boss. They rarely can say "yes" to a project but can almost always cause a "no" if not circumvented.

Note

1. For the historical proof and details from records at the time, see Diarmaid MacCulloch, *Christianity: The First Three Thousand Years* (Viking, 2011).

Chapter

6

In the Buyer's Office

I applied to only two colleges in high school. I was a terrific student with all kinds of accomplishments and offices held, and I was pretty arrogant. Rutgers accepted me, but Columbia required an interview and rejected me. And well they should have.

I absolutely bombed the interview, unprepared, inarticulate, and totally stunned.

Fortunately, Rutgers was and is a great university, and I received a wonderful education, but only because I had a second "buyer." You won't in most cases. You can't afford to be a stumbling, bumbling me when you enter the buyer's office.

So listen up: I'm about to save you a lot of time and grief, providing you pay attention.

> **Alanism**
> Not matter what anyone tells you, you only get to make one first impression.

Establishing Trust

This is a relationship business, and relationships are built on trust. Trust is the firm belief in the reliability and truth of someone, without qualification or hesitation.

You establish trust by being honest, candid, and conversational. You offer *value* (not methodology, but ideas) and actively listen to the buyer. You can establish trust—or at least its beginnings—in the first 10 or 15 minutes of a meeting with a prospect. Or, you may be unable to do so in several meetings. The difference depends on your discipline and focus.

We've already discussed the need for a peer mentality. Thus, the person you're meeting with is evaluating whether you can be of help, *and you should be evaluating whether you choose to be of help*. This is not a win/lose proposition, but rather the determination of whether it can be win/win.

Assuming an hour has been set aside for your meeting, your rough time frame should be:

Establish trust:	10–15 minutes
Finding appropriate issues:	10–15 minutes
Gaining conceptual agreement:	10–15 minutes
"Pouring concrete":	10–15 minutes

Therefore, in 45–60 minutes you should be in a position to submit a proposal in the next day or so with the commitment of the buyer to consider it and give you an answer immediately thereafter. If that sounds aggressive, it is. This business is not for false humility or great deliberation. The longer things take, *the more negative issues are likely to surface*. No buyer ever took three weeks with one of my proposals with the result of requesting that I raise my fees!

How do you establish trust that quickly? Here are the behaviors and traits to consider:

- *Be on time and be well groomed.* Stop in the rest room to ensure that your hair is combed, makeup is applied well, there's nothing stuck in your teeth, buttons and zippers are correctly secured, and so forth. Make sure you have a recent manicure and that your shoes are shined and not scuffed.

- *Don't be a packhorse.* Leave your luggage and anything else you're carrying in the reception area. I prefer to walk in with simply something to take notes. Don't open up a computer, never record the conversation (even with permission, because it tends to make people more cautious), and never, never use a slideshow.

- *Smile, use a firm handshake, and wait to be told where to sit before doing so.* I tend to use "Mr." or "Ms." or "Dr." until I'm told, "Please call me Joan." Then I say, "I'm Alan."

- *Politely refuse any offer of a drink.* Tell the buyer to feel free to go ahead, but that you're fine. The chances of spilling something are simply not worth it, and you're certainly not dying of thirst.

- *Use conversational language and behavior.* Act as if you're having a casual conversation with a friend after work.

- *Be prepared for the opening question or comment.* This will be along the lines of "What can I do for you?" or "What can you do for us?" or "I've heard good things about you" or "Why don't you tell me something about yourself?"

- *Answer briefly.* And then *turn the conversation around* by asking a question in return: "I'm not sure what, if anything, I can do for you! Why don't you tell me what your greatest priorities are at the moment?"

- *Pivot any question, once answered, into a return question.* You should be talking less than 25 percent of the time. (See some of the questions to ask in Appendix A.)

Trust is established in peer-to-peer conversation and comment. You'll find that some buyers prefer to get right down to business, but others are far more sociable ("How long have you been in consulting?" or "Do you enjoy living in Manhattan?"). The important metric here is to know when you've established sufficient trust to move on to discussing issues.

You have probably established a trusting relationship when these conditions are present:

- The buyer doesn't allow for interruptions by phone, text, or the assistant. He or she is not glancing at the computer screen.
- Confidential issues are shared: "This isn't widely known, but we're going to be moving into online sales. Is that something you can help us implement?"
- Humor is used. The buyer offers a funny story, or smiles readily, or responds well to something funny you point out.
- You're asked for advice: "How would you handle a 15-year veteran who has been very important to us but refused to become expert in the technology we're now implementing?"
- The buyer isn't watching the clock and might even say, "I know we set aside an hour, but if you have the time, I'm not concerned about it. I'd like to make sure I learn what I need to know."

Trust is the foundation of the house. Nothing will stand on a weak foundation. *This is the marketing business, essentially, and smart marketing is based on trusting relationships.* We talked about brands earlier, and one of their great benefits is that they are a symbol of trust because they represent salutary past experiences. This first buyer meeting (you only get the chance for one first impression) is your opportunity to begin that branding process with any given buyer.

Remember, you can't leave any poorer than when you arrived. No one will take your money, and if you don't have the opportunity to move forward, at least you will have learned something. There is no giant lever, as in cartoons, that the buyer can pull to open a trapdoor underneath your feet. Just as you have (and everyone else has), that buyer has concerns about family, finances, relationships, job priorities, health, and a myriad of other normal human issues.

It's not too much to ask that you spend a quarter hour or less focused on establishing a solid relationship with the buyer. It's tempting to go into a sales pitch or to be opportunistic and jump on something said like a wrestler intent on pinning the issue to the mat and scoring.

But you're not going to build your business acting as though you're selling computers or paving for the parking lot. What you're providing is value, and that starts with valuable relationships.

Finding Issues and Dynamic Capture

The second of the four parts of the buyer meeting should be geared to finding issues you can address. Now that you've established trust, it should be easier for the buyer to share key issues.

Don't ask the hackneyed, "What keeps you up at night?" Many, if not most, of the organizations and ideal buyers you'll be visiting are successful. (Successful organizations have money, and you want to work with people who can pay you, not people needing remedial help who have no money.) Instead, ask questions such as these:

- *If the board gave you a million dollars to invest in your operation, what would you do with it?* (No one would say that things are perfect and return the money!)

- *If you could change only one thing tomorrow, but it was guaranteed to change, what would you choose?*

- *What do you find yourself spending most of your time on? Would you like to spend still more or less time on it?*

You get the idea: ask interactive, qualitative questions to help determine what the buyer's priority issues are. Now, here is the key about going to the next phase of the conversation (*conceptual agreement*): *You need to keep the conversation headed in the direction you intend to travel.* That is, you can't allow the buyer to dissemble, or ramble, or change the subject. And don't feel that you must be polite and never interrupt. I call this the "boat channel" approach to keeping things on track.

At amusement parks they have boat rides for small children, and while the kids think they can steer (and sometimes are able to do so)

FIGURE 6.1:   The boat channel.

there is a stream propelling the boats forward, and the walls act as guides, so that the boats always wind up where they're supposed to be at the end of the ride (see Figure 6.1).

You have to maintain the boat in this channel by constantly focusing the conversation on key issues with which you can help. You interrupt as needed by saying:

- *Excuse me, but am I correct that you've now mentioned retention as a top priority several times?*
- *May I quickly summarize at this time, to make sure I'm capturing your points? You've said the cross-selling and referral business are the keys to increased revenues.*
- *May I interrupt? Is the real issue here one of creating a common technology?*

These are paraphrases and summaries that enable you to focus on the right journey—the channel—to the desired end: moving into step three, conceptual agreement.

You are seeking in this 10–15 minute portion of the meeting to identify those buyer needs that fit best with your value proposition and skills. In other words, what is the greatest benefit you can bring to the greatest client priority?

> **Alanism**
> You're not in the buyer's office to be liked; you're there to be respected. Small talk has to be overcome with expertise, opinion, and insight.

The idea is to determine which client needs best fall into your value "baskets" (bottom of Figure 6.2). Your baskets may be retention, change, leadership, innovation, and so forth. The more buyer concerns are in any of those baskets, the more powerful your eventual proposal will be. That's why you have to keep the buyer focused on issues with which you can best help.

The ultimate position is what I call *dynamic capture*. Instead of merely hoping to uncover client needs that fit into your existing baskets, *you create a basket to encompass those needs as they are discussed*. I call this "dynamic capture" because you've created a huge, highly important basket right on the spot!

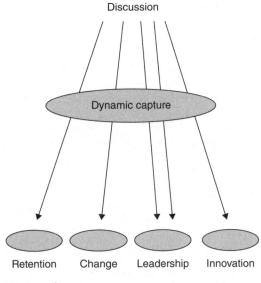

FIGURE 6.2: Dynamic capture.

In the example in the illustration, dynamic capture might be "strong leadership that retains talent, fosters innovation, and anticipates and exploits change." Now you're the solution to the buyer's priorities!

Gaining Conceptual Agreement

"Conceptual agreement" means just that: you and the buyer agree in concept on what's to be accomplished. This is *the* key element in creating a high-fee proposal. You pursue conceptual agreement for consulting projects, not for speeches, for which a letter of agreement would suffice. Nor would you use conceptual agreement for a trusted advisor relationship where you are on retainer in return for "access to your smarts" for a given period of time.

We pursue the three steps of conceptual agreement in consulting projects, which are engaged in solving a problem, or making an improvement, or coaching a key person.

There are three vital steps in conceptual agreement, which in turn is based on trust and the identification of issues, above. (You are now in the third 10–15 minute segment of our hypothetical hour meeting.)

Objectives

Objectives are *business outcomes.* They are never internal goals solely. For example, "creating a happier workforce" is a worthless objective unless it is reflected in happier customers spending more money and raising profitability. You'll find feel-good objectives among HR people, which is why you must speak only to buyers and send proposals only to buyers. A proposal should have about three to six objectives, which are to be met if the project is to be deemed successful.

Here are 10 questions to ask (to the extent needed) to elicit objectives from a buyer:

1. What is the ideal outcome you'd like to experience?
2. What results are you trying to accomplish?

3. What better product/service/customer condition are you seeking?

4. Why are you seeking to do this (work/project/engagement)?

5. How would the operation be different as a result of this work?

6. What would be the ROI (sales, assets, equity, and so forth)?

7. How would image/repute/credibility be improved?

8. What harm (for example, stress, dysfunction, turf wars, and the like) would be alleviated?

9. How much would you gain on the competition as a result?

10. How would your value proposition be improved?

This isn't an interrogation, and these questions are meant as guides for you. Practice "questioning to a void": meaning, ask "What else?" until a category is exhausted—for example, "What *other* results?" or "What other gains?"

There are tangible objectives (increase in sales), intangible objectives (higher repute in the marketplace; see Chapter 8 for more on tangible and intangible objectives), and the buyer's personal objectives (better positioned for promotion, gain more budget and power). Include them all.

Once you've established the outcomes for your project, move on to step two in conceptual agreement.

Measures of Success

These are often called "metrics" and represent *indicators of progress and/or completion*. How will you and the buyer truly *know* that something is being accomplished?

Some of these can be empirical: weekly sales reports, monthly attrition reports, expense calculations, and so forth. Some of these can be anecdotal: the buyer reports she has to play referee among teams less or that meetings are less frequent.

Measures of success should be agreed upon at the outset in the proposal so that it's clear not only that progress is being made *but also that your intervention is accounting for it.*

Here are another 10 questions to ask:

1. How will you know we've accomplished your intent?
2. How, specifically, will the operation be different when we're done?
3. How will you measure this?
4. What indicators will you use to assess our progress?
5. Who or what will report on our results (against the objectives)?
6. Do you already have measures in place you intend to apply?
7. What is the rate of return (on sales, investment, and so forth) that you seek?
8. How will we know the public, employees, and/or customers perceive it?
9. Each time we talk, what standard will tell us we're progressing?
10. How would you know it if you tripped over it?

Alanism
Objectives, measures, and value will set you apart from the competition in every proposal but are reliant on a trusting relationship with a true buyer.

The final step is missing in almost all consulting proposals: an expression of impact or value.

Value

Value is the impact of meeting the objectives. What is the consequence of achieving lower expenses, higher profit, less attrition, or more referrals? You may think that these objectives constitute value in themselves, but let's look more closely.

An example would be "profit." It would seem obvious that higher profits, as an objective, would also be important value. But ask yourself and your buyer, "What would higher profits enable you to achieve?" and you'll be able to develop value such as this:

- Pay down debt
- Expand facilities
- Hire more people
- Pay higher bonuses
- Invest in research and development
- Contribute to the community
- Attract more investment

So you can see that the simple result "profit" actually can be expressed in terms of far greater value! *This is essential, because value constitutes the return on investment that can justify high fees.*A $100,000 fee may sound like a lot, but it's minor compared to a million dollars in savings (which is a 10:1 return ratio).

Now, here's the secret: You should try to have *three* value statements for each objective, and at least half of that total should be monetized. So if you have 5 objectives, you should have 15 value statements and seven or eight should be monetized (that is, showing a specific financial improvement). If the value is going to be reduction in attrition, for example, find out how much it costs to replace each person voluntarily leaving the company. (Buyers know these things or can make intelligent estimates.)

Here are 10 more questions to ask:

1. What will these results mean for your organization?
2. How would you assess the actual return (ROI, ROA, ROS, ROE, etc.)?
3. What would be the extent of the improvement (or correction)?
4. How will these results impact the bottom line?

5. What are the *annualized* savings (first year might be deceptive)?

6. What is the intangible impact (e.g., on repute, safety, comfort, etc.)?

7. How would you, personally, be better off or better supported?

8. What is the scope of the impact (on customers, employees, vendors)?

9. How important is this compared to your overall responsibilities?

10. What if this fails?

Without this conceptual agreement step encompassing objectives, measures, and value, you will never have the basis for a comprehensive, high-value proposal that is consistent with the buyer's personal goals.

Now, before you leave the office, it's time to "pour concrete" on what you've worked so hard to put together. This is, fittingly, the final 10–15 minutes of our one-hour meeting.

Pouring Concrete

In the final 10–15 minutes of your meeting, you should seek to solidify, confirm, and ensure that you and the buyer indeed agree on the objectives, metrics, and, especially, the value. I call this "pouring concrete" to secure a solid foundation before building upon it.

So why not hit the ground zooming?

Bear in mind that this is the rare profession in which we use our past *to improve the client's future* (Table 6.1). But don't make the mistake of charging for your past or methodology: charge only for your contribution to the client's future. That's what to emphasize when you're pouring concrete.

This may take different forms based on your client and market. For example, in most cases with small businesses and SMEs, the buyer's

TABLE 6.1 The unique dynamic of successful consulting

Consultant's past	Competency/ methodology	Client's future
Experiences	Observation	Larger sales
Education	Workshops	Higher retention
Victories and defeats	Facilitation	Lower attrition
Travel	Coaching	Reduced stress
Socialization	Manuals	Better communication
Collaborations	Training	Faster responsiveness
Socialization	Focus groups	Larger market share
Problem solving	Systems and procedures	Enhanced image
Decision making	Conflict resolution	Greater safety
Planning	Negotiating	Higher quality
Innovation	Confrontation	Reduced expenses
Other	Other	Other
Consultant raw material	Consultant transfer mechanism	Client results

partner or spouse will play a role in the decision. As we discussed earlier, this is a highly emotional decision since the investment is perceived as taking money away from other personal needs.

Consequently, you would need to ask questions like these 10, which you wouldn't be asking in a Fortune 1000 firm:

1. Have you arrived at a budget or investment range for this project?

2. Are funds allocated, or must they be requested?

3. What is your expectation of investment required?

4. So we don't waste time, are there parameters to remain within?

5. Have you done this before, and at what investment level?

6. What are you able to authorize during this fiscal year?

7. Can I assume that a strong proposition will justify proper expenditure?

8. How much are you prepared to invest to gain these dramatic results?

9. For a dramatic return, will you consider a larger investment?

10. Let's be frank: What are you willing to spend?

Alanism

After conceptual agreement, don't pat yourself on the back and run down the hall to spend the money. Stay put, and start pouring concrete.

It's best to ask such questions candidly, while you're present, instead of hearing an unfavorable response when you follow up on your proposal!

The following 10 questions represent what you should be asking of *everyone* once conceptual agreement is reached:

1. Is there anything we haven't discussed that could get in the way?

2. In the past, what has occurred to derail potential projects like this?

3. What haven't I asked you that I should have about the environment?

4. What do you estimate the probability is of our going forward?

5. Are you surprised by anything I've said or that we've agreed upon?

6. At this point, are you still going to make this decision yourself?

7. What, if anything, do you additionally need to hear from me?

8. Is anything likely to change in the organization in the near future?

9. Are you awaiting the results of any other initiatives or decisions?

10. If I get this proposal to you tomorrow, how soon will you decide?

If you've developed a truly trusting relationship, asking just a few of these questions should result in a very firm commitment and no surprises later. Don't forget, the buyer has not yet seen any fees (which will appear in your proposal).

If you have the courage and the time to push still further, try these 10 questions as well:

1. Would you be amenable to my providing a variety of options?

2. Is this the only place (division, department, geography) applicable?

3. Would it be wise to extend this through implementation and oversight?

4. Should we plan to also coach key individuals essential to the project?

5. Would you benefit from benchmarking against other firms?

6. Would you also like an idea of what a retainer might look like?

7. Are there others in your position with like needs I should see?

8. Do your subordinates possess the skills to support you appropriately?

9. Should we run focus groups/other sampling to test employee reactions?

10. Would you like me to test customer response at various stages?

Finally, you're approaching the finish line, so you need to practice what my high school track coach taught me to win every close sprint:

run *through* the tape; don't let up as you reach it. So here's how to aggressively go for the close:

1. If the proposal reflects our last discussions, how soon can we begin?

2. Is it better to start immediately or wait for the first of the month?

3. Is there anything at all preventing our working together at this point?

4. How rapidly are you prepared to begin once you see the proposal?

5. If you get the proposal tomorrow, can I call Friday at 10 for approval?

6. While I'm here, should I begin some of the preliminary work today?

7. Would you like to shake hands and get started, with the proposal to follow?

8. Do you prefer a corporate check or to wire the funds electronically?

9. May I allocate two days early next week to start my interviews?

10. Can we proceed?

You've now spent a hypothetical 45–60 minutes in the buyer's office, gaining trust, identifying and capturing issues, establishing conceptual agreement, and pouring concrete. You may find that you have more or less time, or you need more than one meeting.

In general, I've found that if you can't complete this sequence within two hour-long meetings, you're probably not going to do it at all. You must move assertively and rapidly, controlling the conversation: remember the maxim that language controls discussion, which controls relationships, which control business. Keep this in mind:

- State at the outset what your goals are for the meeting and ask what the buyer's goals are.

- Have minimum and maximum (min/max) objectives for yourself, where the minimum is to gain trust and identify issues for a scheduled next meeting, and the maximum is to pour concrete and gain agreement to submit a proposal.
- Interrupt politely if the buyer wanders or rambles. Keep the boat in the channel.
- Summarize and paraphrase frequently.
- Take notes of the key issues, objectives, metrics, and value.
- Focus on three value statements per objective, with half of that total being monetized.

Finally, *always establish an action, time, and date to follow*. For example, "I'll have the proposal in front of you tomorrow, and we'll talk the day after at 10 on your cell phone to determine which option you'll pursue."

Now we can move on to submitting a proposal that's accepted every time.

Chapter 6 Definitions

Dynamic capture: Articulating the buyer's various needs in terms of one overarching goal so that you become the solution to the buyer's priority issues *and not another priority competing against them.*

Conceptual agreement: The arrangement between the consultant and the buyer that reflects common belief in the objectives, measures, and value of the project.

Objectives: Business and personal (for the buyer) outcomes expected of the project.

Measures of success: Metrics that indicate progress and/or completion of the objectives.

Value: The expression of the worth of meeting each of the objectives, both in financial (monetization) and intangible (emotional) terms.

Chapter

Closing the Sale

Aconsulting proposal is a summation, not an exploration. That is, it is *not* a negotiating document, because it is based on previously established conceptual agreement. Therefore, your proposal will have a very high likelihood of acceptance. My own experience is over 80 percent, though people in my communities have claimed over 90 percent.[1]

How to Write a Proposal That's Accepted Every Time

Your proposal should be about 2.5 pages in length. You don't include credentials, résumés, or any collateral information, *because trust has already been established*. There are nine segments in the proposal.

1. Situation Appraisal

This is a paragraph of about 5 to 10 sentences explaining why you've met with the buyer and why this proposal is being submitted. *It is not general background or history.*

Poor: *The Acme Company is a 15-year-old enterprise supplying precise measuring equipment to oil field exploration. It has expanded by 50 percent in the past two years, and is now focusing on offshore exploration for the first time.* The buyer knows all this! It's irrelevant.

Good: *The Acme Company's 50 percent growth rate and expansion into offshore exploration has created the need for an additional 100 engineers in a zero unemployment marketplace, and at least half must possess deep-ocean experience. The challenge is to hire such people from competitors and others without a major disruption to the company's compensation strategy.* That will have the buyer nodding in agreement because that's precisely what you discussed in person.

2. Objectives

3. Measures of Success

4. Value

These are taken verbatim from your conversation in the buyer's office. I prefer bullet points for each:

Objectives

- Identify and hire credentialed and experienced engineers.
- Minimum exceptions to compensation guidelines.
- Hire at least half in the next 90 days.
- Other

Measures of Success

- Candidates approach us having heard about our need.
- We interview at least 10 candidates per week.
- Our own employees informally recruit.
- Other

Value

- We will be able to accept five additional assignments worth $5 million.

- We will save over $150,000 in search fees.
- Our current operations will be minimally disrupted.
- Other

To summarize, proposal steps 2, 3, and 4 are a verbatim description of conceptual agreement.

5. Methodology and Options

This is where you provide the buyer with options. If you provide too many, the buyer may be paralyzed with indecision. If you provide only one, then the proposal is "take it or leave it."

A choice among options will raise your chances of success hugely. I recommend three, in escalating degree. For example:

> **Alanism**
> Providing options enables the buyer to move beyond "Should I do this?" to "*How* should I do this?"

Option 1: Backstage

I will personally coach you and executives you nominate to create attractive job descriptions and use all contacts to reach out to appropriate candidates. I will also work with your human resources team to set up screening that minimizes or eliminates the chances of poor candidates from reaching your executives and taking up their time with irrelevant interviews.

Option 2: Direction

In addition to option 1, I will create a template to use so that all interviews elicit and track identical information, reducing the likelihood of uneven assessments. I will also ensure that diversity is sought and achieved in examining potential candidates, irrespective of gender, race, origins, religion, and other factors of legal and ethical import.

Option 3: Oversight

In addition to option 2, I will personally sit in to audit some interviews and readjust our plans as appropriate and if necessary. I will also create and help implement a rapid assimilation program that will include mentoring for the new people by some of your veteran engineers.

Thus, the first option will meet all the objectives, which is ethically mandatory. But the second and third options offer additional value that can result in higher fees, as you'll see below. *Note that each option is inclusive of the previous option.*

6. Timing

Here you indicate approximate timing for each option, not in calendar days (March 3) because there may be delays in the execution of the proposal, but in relative days:

Option 1 will require about 30 days; option 2, 45–60 days; and option 3, about 90 days.

Note that giving ranges instead of firm dates will provide you with much more flexibility.

7. Joint Accountabilities

Here you specify what you, the client, and both of you together are responsible for. Note that this is a critical aspect of the proposal *because as a consultant you have accountabilities but no authority.* Only the client can make things happen, especially in overcoming resistance.

My Accountabilities

- Meet all agreed upon deadlines
- Debrief you about progress at least every two weeks
- Keep all company matters confidential and sign nondisclosure forms
- Return all calls, emails, and other communications within 24 hours

- Submit expenses promptly at the end of each month

Your Accountabilities

- Keep all agreed upon meetings and calls as a priority
- Provide access to key people and documentation rapidly
- Provide an onsite office and minor administrative support
- Provide security access as needed
- Confine to the company my intellectual property and trademarks
- Ensure payment of all invoices for fees and expenses on due dates

Our Joint Accountabilities

- We mutually agree to immediately inform the other of any developments that might materially affect the success and/or outcome of this project.

This last bullet point is quite important. I've found on occasion that several key people were attempting to leave the company and that there was unreported theft in the warehouses. One buyer neglected to inform me that the division in which the work was being done was going to be divested in the near future!

8. Terms and Conditions

This is my favorite part of the proposal, *where the buyer sees the fees for the first time*. The intent here is that the buyer has been nodding agreement with all the prior reporting, has found an option to his or her liking, and will keep agreeing right through the fees!

State them simply:

- The fee for option 1 is $180,000
- The fee for option 2 is $195,000
- The fee for option 3 is $215,000

If you're curious about these fees, go back and do the math based on the monetized value above. You'll find this hypothetical buyer's return on investment is in the order of almost 30:1! *Your fees should represent a huge ROI for the buyer and equitable compensation for you.* Remember that sentence if a buyer ever asks why you're not charging by the hour or day and what your fee basis is.[2]

Then you offer terms:

- Our terms are 50 percent on acceptance and 50 percent in 15 days for option 1 and 45 days for options 2 or 3. Additionally, we offer a courtesy discount of 10 percent if the full fee is paid upon acceptance of this proposal.

- Expenses will be due monthly as actually accrued and are due on the presentation of our statement.

Note that you *never* want to offer net 30 or some arrangement like that, because the client will then take 60 days. As I've mentioned earlier, some large companies unethically require payment to be made after 120 days, harming their suppliers, and your proposal should override such internal policies (which is why you deal with a buyer and not procurement). Make sure you bill your expenses promptly, or your cash flow will suffer.

Never agree to be paid upon completion, or someone may find reasons to claim the project is not complete (we call this "scope creep").

9. Acceptance

My proposals also serve as a contract. We don't want legal boilerplate in them because they'll then go to the client's legal department and disappear while those lawyers try to prove why they should be on the payroll. Therefore, have a space for your name, title, and date, and the buyer's name, title, and date. Have a box to be checked for the option they select and the payment method they select (in full or in installments). *Note that in many companies, any offer of a discount MUST be accepted!*

Finally, include this sentence: *Your initial payment or full payment will also serve as approval of this proposal in lieu of a signature.* You want to include that in case the buyer just wants to pay you and begin and not send this to legal!

Case in Point

I was hired by a large New York insurance company to help with the aftermath of a huge merger. The option chosen was $250,000, half due on acceptance and half due in 45 days.

The payments took place without any problem, but the proposal was never signed. I finally asked the buyer why that was.

"I have authority to write $125,000 checks," he told me, "but not to sign contracts. If I sent this to legal, God knows what would have happened, so I simply wrote the checks."

Which is why my wording above, is, in effect: *Your payment is as good as your signature!*

Why Buyers Go Dark

More often than it should ever happen, a proposal is submitted with the consultant believing he or she conformed with everything described thus far, yet the buyer won't return phone calls or emails after the proposal is submitted.

I call this *going dark*. There are reasons for it, most of which would be your fault.

There are few greater disappointments than submitting a proposal and then the buyer not returning your calls or emails. I've found it more acceptable for a buyer to actually refuse the proposal so that I can learn what I might have done better in the process. But to hear nothing at all after spending time on the relationship? That's pretty harsh.

Let me prepare you now: here's what might account for a buyer going dark on you after you've submitted the proposal per agreement:

1. This Wasn't a Buyer

You checked and asked all the right questions, but you didn't really do a qualitative analysis. So someone who has an impressive title and decent office played you along. It might be that they could purchase less expensive services and didn't want to admit to you—when they found out your fees—that they hadn't been entirely truthful. The moral here: spend whatever time is needed to ensure you're with a buyer with sufficient budget for your "floor" fees.

2. There Was No Real Trust

We sometimes rush into a sales pitch and don't take the time for the most fundamental and critical step. If my 10–15 minute guideline above is not working for you on occasion, then simply extend it. Don't think, "Well, time to move on!" Revisit the trust indicators above and ensure you're experiencing them.

3. You Read the Signs Wrong

I will guarantee you that whenever you're asked for a proposal more quickly and/or with fewer questions than you had anticipated, the real reason is to get you out of the office. Some buyers don't like to say "no" or don't like to even question candidly: "I'm not sure how this can help me; can you explain that?" Instead, they think the easiest way to dispense with you is to give you overwhelmingly good news! So they'll ask for a proposal and will never take your call again. Don't be too shy to say, "I think a proposal is premature; we haven't really discussed all the pros and cons of such a project."

4. The Objectives Are Not Business Outcomes

This is what I call "the HR proposal," in that the intent is to make everyone happy, but if the business improves, it's just an accident. Don't proceed through conceptual agreement as if it's a checklist to be completed. This step is *qualitative, not quantitative*. Make it apparent how the business will be far better off after you walk away at the conclusion of the project.

5. The ROI Is Weak

If you haven't monetized the value from reaching the objectives (we said three value statements from every objective and half of that total monetized), then you won't have sufficient monetary advantages—at least 10:1—to make the investment justified in the eyes of the investor taking the risk.

6. You're Not a High Enough Priority

Remember that money and time are *priorities and not resources*. You can't be seen as still another priority that the buyer has to move around his or her desk. You have to be viewed as *the remedy that resolves all the other priorities and issues*. You're not a competitor with other issues; you're the solution to them.

7. You've Omitted the Action/Date/Time Step

Never accept "Let's talk in a week" or "I'll get back to you after my trip." You need to confirm: Tuesday at 10 on a Zoom call you'll initiate (or whatever). You must get on the buyer's calendar for the follow-up.

8. You're Slothful

Using my format above, you should be able to create a proposal within an hour or so, and therefore submit it to the buyer within 24 hours. You can then talk the day after that, or about 48 hours after the original meeting. If you wait longer than that for any reason, you're jeopardizing your chances of a positive response (or any response at all).

Alanism

The longer you wait, the more bad things are likely to happen. Act with alacrity. After all, this is about dramatically improving the client's business.

9. Insufficient Concrete

You didn't press enough in that final 10–15 minutes of the meeting to ensure that there were no concerns, questions, conflicting priorities, or other issues that needed addressing while you were present.[3] Insufficient concrete won't hold up a building and won't prompt a return phone call because other issues have overwhelmed yours.

So be forewarned: you can effectively prevent clients from going dark, and it's usually completely within your power to do so. If this happens to you once, it may be you; it may be the buyer. If it happens more than once a year, it's you.

You're Actually Closing Three Sales; Don't Lose Two

One of the secrets of early acceleration in your business is to view a sale as a three-dimensional opportunity. Every sale has three sources of income:

1. The immediate business, supported by the fees and terms stipulated in your proposal
2. Referral business, which delighted clients will provide for you if asked properly, and sometimes even voluntarily

Alanism

We often work hard to close business but then only profit through a third of the potential. Imagine enjoying only a third of your vacation or gaining only a third the value of medication!

3. Expansion business, which is additional business through new projects with the same buyer

We've discussed closing the business through proposals based on trusting relationships with high ROI and options for the buyer to consider moving forward. Here are the other two dimensions to bear in mind from the outset.

Referrals

You should begin seeking referrals about two-thirds of the way through a project, *not at its conclusion.* This is because at this point the buyer has seen dramatic progress, realizes you're delivering what your promised, and is better off through your intervention. You also have the opportunity to frequently talk with the buyer. At the conclusion of a project, that interaction will disappear, or at least diminish sharply.

Figure 7.1 shows the dynamic of referral business sources and uses. *Always* ask for a referral with these criteria in mind:

1. Ask during a normal discussion, preferably in person.

2. Ask for a particular person or position (see the examples below). Never ask, "Who do you know?"

3. Ask with an emotional appeal that is win/win/win.

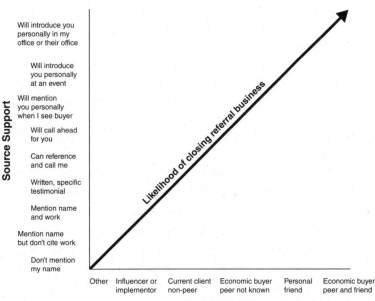

FIGURE 7.1: Referral business dynamic.

Hence, your language should be:

> *Jane, referrals are the lifeblood of my business, and at this point with a successful project, I always ask my client who else could benefit from the value I'm providing you. For example, Henry James is your counterpart for the West Coast, and I'm wondering if you could introduce me so that I could see him when I'm in San Francisco. Also, you've mentioned that your largest supplier is highly innovative and likes to emulate what you're doing here. Could you introduce me to the CEO?*

Notice that in the first case I mentioned a specific *name* and in the second case a specific *position*. There should be no reason at all to deny a request like this, with the appeal of the importance (lifeblood) for your business. (If you don't believe that, by the way, consider that entire professions, such as real estate, insurance, and auto sales are almost entirely based on referral business. Your client's business may also be referral sensitive.)

If you client says for any reason, "Let me think about it," ask immediately if there's a problem with such an introduction.

If your client says, "Give me some material I can forward to them," immediately reply, "I'm not going to put you in the awkward position of marketing for me! I would simply ask that you let them know I'll be calling and that we've worked well together."

If your client says, "Let me just think about whether they're the best people to talk to and get back to you," reply, "Fine, I'll call you Friday at 10 to learn what you advise." (This is the practice of action/date/time.)

If your client says, "I'm not sure when I can reach out to them," reply, "That's no problem, I'll give them a call and mention your name."

The point here is to be highly assertive in eliciting referral business—inside or outside the client company—building on your relationship with the buyer and current success. This is the lowest-cost, fastest way to build new business in any consulting operation, large or small. Ignore it at your peril, because building new business from scratch is time consuming, expensive, and difficult.

Expansion

When you're working within a client's workplace, you have the opportunity to see and hear things beyond the purview of your immediate project. If you handle these issues correctly, you'll get expansion business. If you handle them incorrectly, you'll go broke.

Scope creep occurs when the client asks you to do additional work, beyond the pale of the current proposal, "while you're there." This is akin to your asking the gas station attendant to rotate your tires while he's pumping gas or requesting your insurance agent to also create an estate plan at no extra fee while providing a life insurance policy.

Scope seep occurs when you simply decide to do additional work because it needs being done—even though it has no bearing on your immediate project and proposal—and you want to be useful or appreciated.

Engaging in either of these practices is a sign of low self-worth and an intent to be liked (rather than respected). Scope creep and scope seep will cost you time and profits and will often undermine the existing project by conflating the results of disparate issues.

The language for the client is: "I'd be happy to help with this additional priority. Let me write an addendum to our current proposal (or create a new proposal)." The language for expansion business is to resist scope seep and pivot the scope creep in the right direction.

Here is the vital language to use:

> *As a consultant, I have the benefit of observing and learning in your company beyond the scope of my immediate project. I've discovered three issues that I think merit your attention, and they may be things you can resolve on your own. However, if you need my help with them, I'd be happy to do so.*

This statement is far more powerful than it looks. It's extended as an objective observer with the client's best interests in mind. It focuses on immediate improvement in important areas. It acknowledges that the client may resolve the issues unilaterally, and therefore there is no quest for business or self-aggrandizement. *However, it also offers help through your services.*

This kind of attitude and this kind of language are key to expanding business, not merely doing more of what you're already doing (which is fine), but in adding to it qualitatively and not merely quantitatively.

This is what completes the third aspect of every sale. And you need to pursue this with every client. Few things will move you further more quickly this early in your consulting career than aggressively pressing for referrals and expansion business.

Case in Point

I was working on a project for a client in Pittsburgh that called for me to wander through the warehouses where, I knew, the company's own executives never ventured. Although I found nothing amiss in terms of my project, I did find a completely inappropriate, old-fashioned pinup calendar of a partially clad woman.

I pointed out to the warehouse manager that this constituted a hostile work environment and it ought to be removed along with all others like it. He replied, "This is a warehouse, not the main office, and it's the way to do things here."

I mentioned this at the end of my scheduled debrief with the company president. He was appalled. He was about to pick up the phone and take care of it when I said to him, "You know, you have three issues here. There's the inappropriate calendar. Then there's the attitude that allowed it to remain there and also perhaps allowed other behavior that is unacceptable. There's the fact that your HR people are asleep at the switch, because they clearly have neither educated all your people about such issues nor implemented any monitoring. And I might also mention that you should think about how rarely your own executive team visits all the disparate parts of your operation."

He put the phone down and said, "I need your help with all of this. Are you willing to take this on in addition to our current work?"

The Virtual Handshake

You don't always need a signed contract to begin work. I mentioned earlier the large project with the buyer who could write a check but couldn't sign my proposal!

In your business environment you'll encounter buyers who are traveling extensively and who are difficult to meet in person after your initial meeting. But you'll also find that every one of them has access to, and uses extensively, technology. They have smartphones, tablets, and laptops. They use Zoom, Skype, GoToMeeting, and probably a couple of things invented while you're reading this.

You do not need a formal signature on your proposal to acquire a contract or to begin work. What you need is a simple "yes."

When you follow up with your buyer after submitting the proposal on an agreed-upon date and time, you should begin with this question, called an "assumptive close": *Which option have you decided to implement?* Simple as that. Don't begin with an inquiry about whether they have questions about the proposal or would like to meet again or anything else. You've already established conceptual agreement, already poured concrete, and in your options and fees have demonstrated value with a huge ROI for your buyer.

Normally, the buyer would sign his or her copy of the proposal and send it back, initiate your payment (either first installment or complete fee with a full-payment discount), and agree on a start date for the first steps of the project (for example, interviews, discussion, observations, survey, and so forth).

An oral agreement[4] *is a contract*. If you're dealing with a true buyer who has budget to fund the project (hence, the earlier steps in finding the true buyer), then his or her approval on the phone, or in an email, or a text, or a Zoom call, or through any similar means is sufficient to proceed. If you need to send an invoice, then send it at that time. But also, start the work.

Therefore, if during your actual meeting prior to the proposal a buyer tells you that he or she will be out of town or indisposed for some period of time, indicate that any of these other options are fine *and set them up.* In other words, an email while visiting Hong Kong is perfectly fine, as is a phone call from the beach. Buyers *never* insulate themselves completely from work, even on vacation, and most planes have Wi-Fi, so there's seldom even a need to wait until they land in order to close the deal!

Alanism
Your buyer is closing business and making sales while traveling, so there's no reason on earth (literally) that you can't be closing business with them!

A real or virtual handshake seals a deal. If you happen to be with a buyer and, without signing the proposal, the buyer shakes on option 2, you have a deal. If you receive a "yes" by phone, or any other means above, you have a deal. All are virtual handshakes.

Digression: The Handshake Test

If you ever want to test whether someone is a real buyer or just pretending to be for ego's sake, try this: "If you're able to fund this project and you're in favor of it, can we shake hands right now and move forward while I'm here and attend to the paperwork later?"

Since a handshake is a legal contract, a nonbuyer will stop the charade at that point.

After you've done the hard work of finding your ideal buyer, establishing trust, building a proposal, and creating high-value options, *don't allow something silly, such as travel or vacation or business meetings, to interfere.* Remember that buyers are carrying on their business daily, attending to their accountabilities regularly, no matter where they are or what they're doing (with the exception of family crises and health issues).

Consequently, I have two more pieces of advice before we move past the virtual handshake:

1. Always build a relationship with the buyer's secretary or administrative assistant (who's usually a secretary with a larger desk). Never treat this person aloofly or as an interference. He or she can give you the lowdown on whether the buyer is on an actual trip or off on a family obligation. That assistant can get you on a calendar and relay messages by other than traditional means.

2. Suggest that the buyer use a proxy for approval. If, indeed, the buyer is going to be sequestered in a board meeting or a governmental study, agree that one of his or her lieutenants can be charged with approving your proposal in the buyer's absence.

We've now done everything possible to ensure acceptance of your proposal. Let's take a look at how to ensure it's accepted with high fees.

Chapter 7 Definitions

Scope creep: The tendency of consultants to agree to requests by the client to do additional work beyond the scope of the proposal with no additional fee.

Scope seep: The tendency of consultants to *suggest* additional work beyond the scope of the proposal with no additional fee.

Going dark: The failure on the part of the buyer to respond to communications of any kind after the proposal is submitted.

Oral agreement: A spoken acceptance of your proposal and/ or a handshake that indicates acceptance of your proposal by the buyer.

Notes

1. For far more detail than we have room for here, see my book *Million Dollar Consulting® Proposals* (John Wiley & Sons, 2011).

2. For a thorough investigation of value-based fees, see my book *Value Based Fees*, 2nd ed. (John Wiley & Sons, 2008).

3. This includes asking about a partner or spouse in a small-business setting and meeting with them.

4. The word "verbal" pertains to anything using words, spoken or written. I'm using "oral" to emphasize a spoken agreement.

Chapter

Paying the Mortgage

We're going to step back into the proposal at this point to understand how to create value-based fees. If you don't do this and you charge like an amateur—by the hour or day—you'll leave six figures on the table every year, *which you'll never, ever be able to recapture.*

Why do that?

How to Establish Value-Based Fees

I pioneered value-based fees for consultants in the late 1980s and popularized them in 1992 in the first edition of *Million Dollar Consulting* (McGraw-Hill, 1992). For those of you who acquired the book you're now reading and turned directly to this section, welcome. May I suggest that, when you're done here, you go back and cover the first seven chapters, which, I'm told, have some important information for success.

Let me repeat this admonition and make it clear: anyone charging for their services in time units is an amateur in consulting. In fact, any

117

Alanism

Since a client is always best served with a speedy resolution to an issue, and consultants who charge in time units are always best rewarded for lengthy work, there is an integral ethical conflict in charging by the hour or day. Not only will you make less money, but you will not be serving your client well.

professionals doing this may be adept at their profession, but they are lousy businesspeople. (Yes, I know lawyers charge in six-minute intervals, and therein is my point. You want legal advice from an attorney, not business advice, believe me.)

You fees should be based on the value you are providing. Some value is tangible for the organization: for example, profit, reduced attrition, higher market share. Some is intangible: being perceived as a better community citizen, a more aesthetic workplace, a better attraction of job candidates.

Some value is personal for the buyer, and tangible: fewer hours worked, reduced stress, more raises and promotions. Some is intangible: higher reputation, better career prospects longer term, more support for positions. In Figure 8.1 I've shown the relationship among the four possibilities, and you can use this as a guide or template when you're actually working with a prospect.

You can never create too much value!

Since we have monetized value from the proposal's objectives in conceptual agreement, and since we have provided options in the proposal, we're in a position to assign a fee to each option *based on that option's contribution to the overall project.* Our contribution is measured by achieving the metrics for progress and success included in conceptual agreement.

You mindset has to be in this orientation. It doesn't matter whether your fee is $155,000 or $170,000, because both represent huge profit for you (the "equitable compensation" I alluded to earlier). However, if you're charging $12,000 for something, $10,000 and $14,000 *do* represent significant differences, so we're talking here of major projects,

FIGURE 8.1: Tangible and intangible value.

not minor work. (Similarly, people charging by the hour sweat over whether they can get $200 or $300, which is ridiculous.) The difference in the large project is 10 percent; in my second example, 20 percent; and in my third example, 50 percent.

Obviously, the more monetization of value in your proposal (the tangibles) the better. My advice is that you try to show a 10:1 return. That is an outstanding return, and far more than people receive short term in almost any nonspeculative, low-risk investment. That's why, when agreeing on monetization, you want to take the *low end* of ranges *and cut monetary estimates in half.* This ensures that your 10:1 return is *very* conservative from the outset.

In the next segment we'll look at specific formulas for creating these fees for each option, but first I'd like to emphasize these requirements for value-based fees. All of them you control:

- Remember that your proposal is a summation and not an exploration. *Never negotiate the fees you set in a proposal, or the buyer will wonder, "How low can we go?"* You can negotiate terms, but never fees, unless you concomitantly remove value from the proposal.

- Prepare an explanation for your fee bases to soothe those only familiar with hourly and daily pricing. See my words above, about equitable compensation in return for dramatic ROI, for example.

- Do not discuss fees with the buyer before presenting the proposal. The language here, if pressed, would be "*It's unfair to you if I quote a figure off the top of my head without seriously reviewing our discussions and objectives. I can have it for you in 24 hours, with options and ROI.* No one needs a fee this minute.[1]

- Use generic value (that is, the value *all* of your clients receive from working with you, irrespective of the particular project— higher productivity, better retention of talent, or whatever) as well as the value intrinsic to that particular client project (for example, create a cross-selling mechanism so that all of our sales people can sell all of our products on any prospect call).

- Practice stating the fee in case you have to talk about it.

Case in Point

I once worked for a brilliant guy who owned a consulting firm in Princeton. At the time, you could smoke cigars in offices. Whenever he and I met with an executive, he had his cigar.

I finally said one day, "Ben, the cigar is kind of rude, isn't it?"

"I need the cigar," he assured me.

"Why?" I asked.

"Because when they ask me the fee for our strategy work and I say '$50,000,' if I don't put the cigar in my mouth I begin to giggle."

Fee Formulas

It's simple to set fees *if* you don't complexify it. The first key we've already covered: gaining buyer commitment to the value of the project (see Figure 8.2).

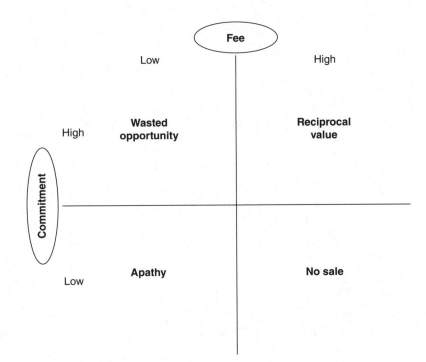

FIGURE 8.2: Buyer commitment and fees.

You want to take advantage of the reciprocal value on the upper right on the chart, where your high fee is justified by the high commitment to value. Too many consultants—even veterans—find themselves in the land of wasted opportunity because they've managed to show great value but become timid in terms of charging commensurate fees for that value.

What those veterans have missed is that, as your career progresses, your brand should build, your approaches should become more and more streamlined, and therefore *your labor intensity diminishes as your fees increase*. This is a dynamic that you can begin laying the groundwork for now, and is shown in Figure 8.3.

Alanism

Just as reducing debt is as important as increasing revenues, decreasing labor is as important as increasing fees. I can always make another dollar, but I can't make another minute.

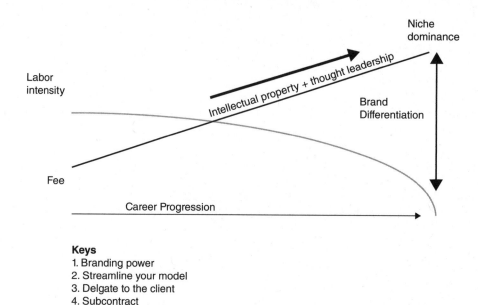

Labor intensity

Fee

Career Progression

Keys
1. Branding power
2. Streamline your model
3. Delgate to the client
4. Subcontract

FIGURE 8.3: Diminishing labor as fees increase.

Another way to look at this is that at the outset, fees follow value, as you might expect. But at a certain point, the lines cross (see Figure 8.4).

What this means is that people expect to get what they pay for. The point at which the lines cross is where your brand is sufficiently strong to convince people that your fees *are expected to be high*, and they place great value in that perception.

Not long ago, I needed a wrench that I didn't own, so I went to the hardware store where there were three identical wrenches from different manufacturers, each about two dollars apart. I chose the most expensive one because I suspected it would be made of better materials and would be more reliable and last longer. Did I research it? No. I assumed the price of the most expensive one was justified by its inherent value.

No one has ever yelled for the cheapest heart surgeon or divorce lawyer or architect. And no executive ever issues a directive such as, "This is a major challenge for us; go out and find me the cheapest consultant!" (HR would try to do that, but I've told you to stay away from HR.)

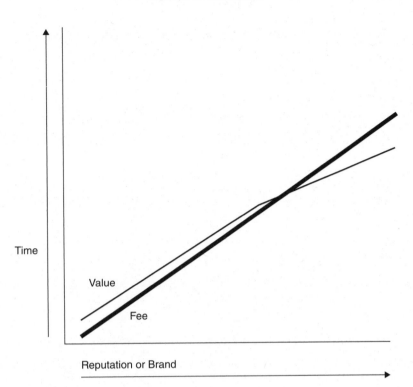

FIGURE 8.4: Value following fee.

Here is a methodical and reliable and highly rewarding formula for establishing your fees:

1. Take the tangible value of the project and annualize it. This means that the cost savings from reduced attrition or more efficient inventory control aren't restricted to this year, but will continue in future years.

2. Add to this the intangible benefits times their emotional impact. If the buyer is tired of playing referee among competing business units or teams and you can eliminate this (or you can reduce the hours required at the office, for example), then consider that as important contributors to fee levels.

3. Add to this peripheral benefits of the project. For example, if you are reducing attrition and improving the work environment, this could result in the need to recruit fewer people,

thereby reducing recruiting costs. In fact, it could result in people coming to the client seeking positions, thereby eliminating recruiting costs, even though the project was about higher employee engagement.

Thus:

$$\frac{\text{Tangible benefits} \times \text{annualization} + \text{Intangible benefits} \times \text{emotional impact} + \text{Peripheral benefits}}{\text{Fees}} = \text{ROI (total value)}$$

$$\frac{\text{Tangible outcomes} \times \text{Expected duration of outcomes} + \text{Intangible outcomes} \times \text{Emotional impact of intangibles} + \text{Peripheral benefits} + \text{Variables positively effected}}{\text{Fixed investment required}} = \text{Client's good deal}$$

Fee setting is part art and part science. The science is in demonstrating 10:1 or better returns on the investment with every option. The art is delineating the impact of both tangible and intangible benefits that can be directly attributable to your project. At high-level fees, you don't have to be exact. And once your brand and word-of-mouth are strong, you don't have to worry about perception.

Right from the outset, as you're getting started, you should be aggressive about fees. Remember that if you leave $50,000 on the table each year, in 10 years you've lost a half-million dollars *that can never be recovered.*

And what if you're leaving $100,000 on the table....

Fifty Factors to Consider

Here is a summary, with some additions, of how to increase your fees on a continuing basis.

1. Establish value collaboratively with the buyer.
2. Consider both tangible and intangible value.
3. Identify personal as well as organizational goals.
4. Stipulate the generic value that all clients receive from you.

5. Identify the peripheral benefits.

6. Never base fees on tasks or deliverables.

7. Never use time as your fee basis.

8. Don't focus on what the buyer wants; focus on what the buyer *needs*.

9. Think of the fourth sale first: fees are cumulative over time.

10. Engage the client in the diagnosis; don't be prescriptive.

11. Never voluntarily offer to reduce fees to overcome resistance.

12. Add a premium if you "personally" do it all.

13. Reduce value if you must reduce fees.

14. Always provide options—a choice of "yeses."

15. Always provide one option over the stated budget.

16. As early as possible, ask, "What is the improved state you seek?"

17. Broaden objectives to provide more potential value.

18. Ensure the buyer is aware of the full range of your services.

19. If there's a small part you can't do, subcontract.

20. Ask why *you're* needed: Why me, why now, why in this manner?

21. Determine if the buyer perceived options other than you.

22. Use your proposal as a confirmation/summation, not negotiation.

23. When asked early about fees, reply, "I don't know at this point."

24. Seek non-fee benefits, such as testimonials and referrals.

25. Reject troublesome, unpleasant buyers.

26. Pay subcontractors on an hourly basis.[2]

27. Anyone you hire must be able to sell new business.

28. Seek out new buyers from your clients while delivering.

29. It's better to work *pro bono* for nonprofits rather than for low fees.

30. Fees have nothing to do with supply and demand, only with value.

31. Ignore others' fees and business models.

32. Psychologically, higher fees imply higher quality.

33. Value is subjective as well as objective.

34. Introduce new value to existing clients to raise existing fees.

35. Don't accept referral business if time-based rates are expected.

36. If phases are needed, extend a discount to begin new phases early.

37. Provide a discount for full payment upon acceptance.

38. Every 18 months consider jettisoning the bottom 15 percent of your clients.

39. Start with payment terms maximally beneficial to you.

40. Do whatever you can to keep proposals out of the legal department.

41. Never agree to payments upon completion of a project.

42. Focus your projects on improvement, not problem solving.

43. Offer proactive ideas and be opportunistic.

44. Practice calmly explaining and stating your fees and their basis.

45. Follow up immediately on overdue payments.

46. Invoice promptly and with payment due on a clear date.

47. Do not deal with accounts payable or procurement, only the buyer.

48. Move clients to the right of the accelerant curve whenever possible.

49. Continually provide unique, new value to existing clients.

50. Always be prepared to walk away from business.

I hope these 50 points give you something to think about and the means to avoid leaving a million bucks on the table.

Remember, too, that *wealth is discretionary time* and a strong brand is what creates that wealth (see Figure 8.5).

Other Fee Considerations

RFPs

You may run into organizations (especially in government, academia, and nonprofits) that require *RFP*s: requests for proposals. These are lengthy "applications" that bid on a piece of prescribed work. They are used to procure computers and snowplows and, unfortunately, professional services.

Their huge weaknesses:

- They are created and administered by nonbuyers: low-level people who look at cost and not value.

> **Alanism**
>
> Clients will not suggest you raise your fees. They will positively respond to higher fees when you provide increased and unique value.

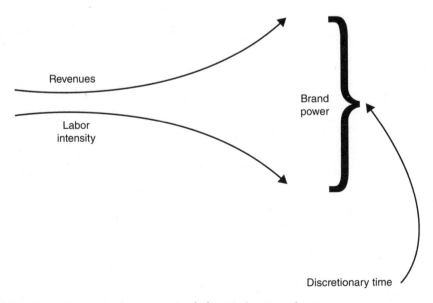

FIGURE 8.5 Brand power and discretionary time.

- They are very detailed and labor-intensive to complete.
- They provide draconian payment schedules and usually demand time-based fee quotes.

The way to avoid these is to:

- Become a sole-source provider. That means that no one else is as appropriate as you for the work. You may have a language capability, a book in print, travel experiences, and so forth that are required, and no one else can match, so competitive bidding is irrelevant.
- Meet the buyer anyway and see if an intended RFP can be designed to suit you more than anyone else. If the buyer is sufficiently sold on you, he or she may be willing to do this.
- Walk away. Even if you win one, it will be on terrible terms and highly labor intensive.

Collaborations

There are times when someone else needs you or you need someone else. For example, you're the expert in organizational design, but there's a financial analysis needed outside of your expertise. It's a considerable portion of the work, so it's more of a partnership than subcontracting.

I look at three parts of the process here: acquisition, methodology, and delivery. Acquiring business is by far the most difficult; methodology is important; and delivery, while also important, can be done by a great many people. Thus, my model:

	Acquisition (50%)	Methodology (30%)	Delivery (20%)
Me			
You			

On a $100,000 sale that I acquire, using your methodology, where we'd split delivery evenly, the chart would look like this:

	Acquisition (50%)	Methodology (30%)	Delivery (20%)
Me	$50,000	$0	$10,000
You	$0	$30,000	$10,000

The total would be $60,000 for me and $40,000 for you. I call this "objective apportionment" because there are clear criteria and an easy breakdown of who earns what. Ask yourself this: Is it hardest to acquire clients, build methodology, or find delivery people? Those aspects are in order of difficulty, so that's the rationale for my apportionment.

Use something like this for true collaborations, never merely for subcontractors, who would not deserve 20 percent for mere delivery.

Retainers

One of the highest revenue and lowest labor relationships you can develop is as a trusted advisor. A *retainer* is the means of payment for such an advisor.

This is not a lawyer's retainer, which is simply a deposit from which is drawn the lawyer's hourly charges. This retainer is a fee paid monthly or quarterly or even annually to ensure priority access to your expertise (your "smarts").

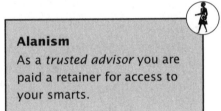

Alanism

As a *trusted advisor* you are paid a retainer for access to your smarts.

There are three aspects to establishing fees for advisory relationships:

1. Who is involved? Is it just the buyer, or the buyer and a few top lieutenants? Generally, it's hard to be a trusted advisor to more than three or four people *in the same organization.*

2. What is the scope? Are you available during Eastern business hours when your client is on the West Coast? Are you available after hours and on weekends? Will you visit on site for certain meetings?

3. What is the duration? How long is this to take place?

This is a vault item on the accelerant curve. If you had 12 of these relationships for a year at $100,000 each, that's $1.2 million in revenue for virtually never leaving home! Yes, some people do this.

My advice is to be paid at least quarterly (an interval of less than a quarter doesn't provide enough time or issues to be of high value) and to give a discount if paid for a longer period at the outset (for example, paid for the entire year when you begin the engagement). *Note that these are not projects, only advice given by email, phone, and other communications vehicles.* Continue to price projects as described in the proposals above. Theoretically, you can have both project work and advisory work with the same client, though it's rare.

Now that you can pay the mortgage, let's see how high you can go.

Chapter 8 Definitions

RFP: Request for proposal, favored by academia, government, nonprofits, and sometimes even for-profit organizations. They focus on delivery and methodology, and are created and administered by low-level people. However, several years ago, the US government FAIR Act stipulated that proposals could be accepted on the basis of value and not solely lowest cost.

Trusted advisor: A consultant, coach, or expert who provides access to their talents and opinions as a sounding board for a stipulated duration of time.

Retainer: The monthly, quarterly, or annual fee device to pay a trusted advisor.

Notes

1. One exception: In the SME marketplace you may well want to say, "The minimum fee for the kind of work we're discussing would be $25,000 for the basic option, moving up to higher value options. Does that present a problem for you?" It's best to do that while pouring cement.

2. Don't mention my books to them.

Moving On Up

I f you're old enough to remember the great comedy *The Jeffersons* or see it on reruns, you know its fabulous theme song, "Movin' On Up." They were moving to a "deluxe apartment in the sky" on the East Side.

Moving up isn't as simple in this profession as climbing a ladder. But the ascent can be rapid and thrilling, or it can be tortuous and frustrating.

Fastening the Watertight Doors

As we grow and progress, we are on an upward journey. Unless we're climbing, we're not growing. If your new venture in consulting makes $75,000 in year one, you certainly don't want to make "only" $80,000 in year two. With your momentum and new clients and continual learning you should double or triple the first year easily.

This is often explained in an *S curve*, which you can see in Figure 9.1. You can achieve dramatic growth as a startup, but the growth will eventually slow and plateau unless you do something to add to it. All plateaus eventually erode because of the laws of entropy, so the best time to leap to the next S curve is when you have strong growth momentum near the top of the hill, not after you've plateaued.

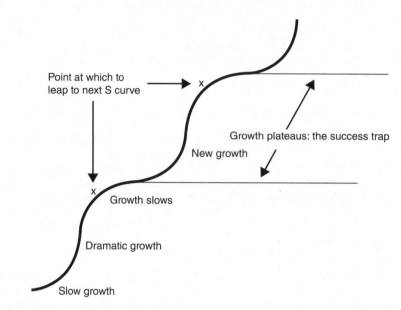

Point at which to
leap to next S curve

x

Growth plateaus: the success trap

New growth

x

Growth slows

Dramatic growth

Slow growth

FIGURE 9.1:   The S curve.

I call these plateaus "success traps," because even though you've grown, you've actually stalled, often without realizing it, and trying to jump from one plateau to the next is a huge expenditure of energy.

So you want to make the leap while you're growing, not while you're coasting. *The only people who can continually coast are those whose vehicles are headed downhill.*

There's another way to view this, and in more detail. I've segmented growth into four stages separated by what I call *watertight doors*. The trouble is that we don't always seal the doors, so we tend to slide back.

The watertight doors are based on a progression of moving from a poverty, or scarcity, mentality to one of abundance.

On the left of Figure 9.2 we see people struggling to survive. We take any business we can to put bread on the table. When I was fired and began my current career, I was doing $25 résumé reviews at one point! I wasn't picky or choosy—I needed income, so long as it was ethical and legal. I call this the "survive" level.

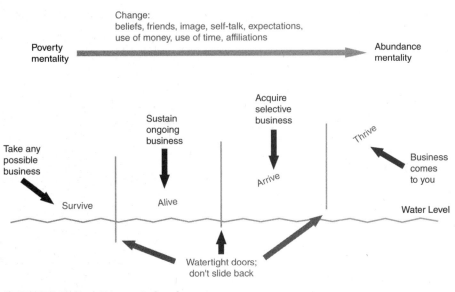

FIGURE 9.2: Watertight doors.

Then we move to "alive." That means we've been able to bring in business, which we now seek to sustain at a certain level of comfort. We have our highs and lows, but we're what accountants would call "a going concern," meaning we're paying bills, supporting our families, and even putting some money aside.

We then progress to the "arrive" level. This is where we can take selective business, focus on ideal buyers, and stop chasing money altogether. Clients often come to us, and referral business is strong.

Finally, we have "thrive," which means that business comes to us regularly, we have a strong brand, we're discriminating in terms of accepting business, and we're considered thought leaders in our field.

The slippage occurs when, despite our movement through these advancing phases, our mentality remains with prior phases. Many people never lose the survivor mentality. They still refuse to spend money, look for the cheapest deals, and view a check on the table as if it's a scorpion about to strike the hand that touches it.

As we move left to right, from poverty to abundance, we have to make changes: among friends, interests, image, self-talk, expectations, standards, affiliations, memberships, and so forth. If we don't keep changing these, it's extremely difficult to seal the watertight doors and prevent our slipping back.

I've had to coach people who, despite making seven figures a year, continued to fly coach on 12-hour flights in order to save some money. Do that often enough, and it can affect your health and certainly your ability to do business. But this isn't just a matter of spending money. An abundance mentality includes:

- Not believing you have to work every waking moment.
- Engaging in hobbies, vacations, volunteerism, and so on.
- Making impulse purchases.
- Looking at value and not cost (as you would expect your clients to do).
- Refusing a client's requested date because it's inconvenient.
- Being philanthropic with advice, time, and money.
- Coaching and mentoring others for free.
- Not feeling guilty about your success.
- Not fearing what others say about you.
- Not needing approval.

> **Alanism**
> True wealth is discretionary time. The more you allow yourself, the wealthier you are.

You need to change your beliefs and mentality in order to continue moving toward an abundance mentality. If you don't change them from when you were just trying to survive, you'll always be in survival mode.

Case in Point

When I was fired in 1985 as president of a consulting firm, I decided to go out on my own so that I had control of my own fate. I also decided to fly first class, wear an excellent suit, and take limos.

My wife asked if this was a good idea, since we had very little money.

I said, "If I'm going to interact as a peer of executive buyers, I have to look successful, and I can't travel so that I'm tired, cramped, perspired, and wrinkled. Besides, these costs are relatively minor, and one sale pays for all of it for a year."

I was right, and here I am.

My advice is to adopt an abundance mentality *early, even prematurely,* so that you are always seen as a success. No one with scuffed shoes or a frayed collar or exhaustion has ever impressed me. These are not conditions one is born with; these are conditions that are accepted and tolerated.

A final story: I flew to London for a meeting, walked off first class and was met by a guide who took me through customs to my limo, which took me to my hotel where I was preregistered and shown immediately to my room. After unpacking, I went to the dining room for dinner.

Over my cocktail, I spotted someone checking in who was to be at the meeting. I invited her to join me and she said she'd be right down. I realized, while waiting, that she had to have been on the same plane, since we would have left from the same city. I found out that she was, but in coach. She had no assistance and took a taxi. She arrived at the hotel 90 minutes after I did.

Count up all those 90 minutes. I talked earlier about not leaving money on the table. Don't leave time on the table either, because you can never recover it.

Alanism
I can always make another buck, but I can't make another minute.

Why You Don't Need a Staff and How to Find Resources

When I was fired, I immediately looked into office space. My wife said to me, "Why do you need an office? You're going out to see people; no one is coming here. If it turns out later that you do need an office, find one then."

That saved me, over a 17-year period, an estimated $450,000 of rent, utilities, insurance, equipment, and so forth. Why did I choose 17 years for my example?

Because I sent both my kids to private schools from kindergarten through undergraduate for a total tuition bill of . . . $450,000.

Are you listening?

Many of you reading this are leaving a career where you had resources at your disposal: equipment, procedures, backups, research, supplies—and most of all, *people*. In fact, in most careers, one sign of success and prestige is how many people work for you.

Well, all ye who enter here, abandon such thinking.

It's really not hard. I wound up managing national and international sales forces for a consulting firm in Princeton early in my other life. I found it demoralizing. Everyone wanted special treatment, victories were theirs but defeats were someone else's fault, and I became so tired of the whining that I posted a sign on my office wall that said, "NO WHINING." When anyone started to moan, I just pointed at the wall.

Working without employees, supervisors, or those to be supervised is a freeing experience. You have to convince yourself that you don't need any people in terms of the business, at least not full-time people.

Alanism

Many of you are refugees from large firms who went out on your own and who now have a tougher boss than ever.

You don't need a secretary or assistant or scheduler. I've always run a multimillion-dollar solo practice by myself. Yet I encounter people making $300,000 a year before taxes who spend $35,000 of it on an assistant.

The basic reason that people hire unneeded assistants—real or virtual—is laziness and sloth. They don't want to make their own travel plans, and don't want to update computer records, hate to manage their own calendars, don't like coordinating times with clients.

Boo hoo.

First, I suggest you overcome the fear. (Procrastination is simply fear. As I've stated, it's a more acceptable fear to tolerate for many people than the fear of actually trying something and not doing it well.) Second, I suggest that all of us *do* need situational help, and here is how to go about it.

Don't Be Available, Be Accessible

Use your phone voice mail and email to respond to people quickly, but never allow any device to interrupt you. When someone's phone rings while we're talking and they look and say, "I have to take this," I simply walk away. That's rude and stupid, assuming you're not an on-call brain surgeon or waiting to hear medical test results.

I return all voice mail within 90 minutes during my regular business hours and all email within a half day. People are delighted with that level of responsiveness, because it's better than 99 percent of all others.

Control your time by not allowing interruptions and scheduling responses according to priorities.

Outsource

You should be outsourcing a wide variety of needs on a situational basis, meaning you pay as needed, whether regularly or irregularly. These include:

- *Bookkeeping.* You can get someone for a few hundred dollars a month to balance your checkbook, prepare a general ledger, provide monthly revenue and profit reports, and so on. My bookkeeper picks up and delivers. Ask your tax accountants for a recommendation if you can't find someone. (Don't use your accountants for this; they'd be way too expensive.) Don't use computer software to keep your own books, no matter whether you have a financial and/or technical background. You need an objective third party.

- *Graphics.* There are all kinds of firms that can create PowerPoint and other types of presentations. Don't spend your time with software that true professionals can utilize better in a tenth of the time.

- *Printing.* There are chain print shops all over that can print on demand, put together booklets, create presentation kits, even print close to a site where you need the finished product.

- *Travel.* Find a good online travel agent who will learn your preferences, use your affinity club numbers, and plot trips for you. I strongly recommend you use American Express, which offers such service for free to Platinum (and Black) Card holders and is available 24 hours a day internationally. They can also book hotels, cars, tours, dinners, and so forth.

- *Taxes.* They say a lawyer has a fool for a client when he represents himself, and I'll tell you that anyone in this business, with the current tax codes, who chooses to file his or her own taxes has a death wish. Find an expert (probably within your accounting firm) who can not only keep you out of jail but also save you some money.

- *Program delivery.* Always subcontract; never keep such people on board as employees. If you do, you'll become an employment agency. One of my clients told me that whenever she returned from a business trip, she knew she'd have her dozen people awaiting "in the nest, chirping like baby birds, waiting to be fed." Do you really want to work and take risks to feed nonfamily members? Subcontractors are available all over, because these are excellent presenters and delivery people who are not good at marketing or are afraid to risk being out on their own, so they need people like you. Pay them by the day, and don't let them near this book.

Assuming you work at home, you don't need any office help. If you've taken a shared space, that is taken care of in your fees. If you feel you need a separate office for which you pay rent (you don't have the room or privacy at home, there is no shared space within a reasonable distance), then become accustomed to working there alone. Answer your own phone. People actually like that. (Do *you* enjoy going through assistants and phone menu selections?)

Hire a cleaning service to come in once a week and keep it simple. But remember that $450,000 I saved, *which in today's money is $723,000.*

Now, I know what a lot of you are thinking: What about resources as I grow? What if I do hire people to sell and deliver?

After my initial response, which is don't do that, my next response it to keep things lean and mean anyway. But I'm warning you here and now as your best resource in this business (this book didn't cost all that much): once you hire people, you have financial obligations, tax burdens, benefit requirements, dangers of appropriation of intellectual property, quality threats, and a huge burden on your time from personal problems, absences, and general whining.

If I make that seem draconian, it's deliberate. It's challenging to create a successful solo practice, so why weigh yourself down with a ton of problems *that you don't really need to succeed brilliantly in your business.*

You once had resources that made your life easier. Now you have freedom that will make your life thrilling. You're in the big time, in the race. Don't run it with 100-pound pack on your back.

Passive Income Alternatives

We discussed passive income near the outset, as a means to begin brand creation and to lure new business. I want to revisit it here as a strategy to implement as you proceed up through the "arrive" and "thrive" levels of the watertight doors.

First, let's define *passive income*:

> *Narrow definition.* The stereotypical definition is "making money while you sleep." This means the sales of products of any type, from formal books to simple guidelines, which people download and purchase. They are either automatically fulfilled via email, or they are fulfilled by you using traditional means.
>
> *Expanded definition.* I favor a broader definition, whereby you are making money without leaving home. You may be interacting with others by phone or over the Internet, or even in person through coaching. My very broad definition is when I'm around my home. I have a retreat center that accommodates a dozen people, and although I'm certainly not sleeping when making money from these programs, I still consider it passive income because there is no travel involved. Before I built the retreat center and I utilized a hotel eight minutes away, I considered that passive income as well, even though I was sometimes addressing over 100 people and "working" for six hours.

I wanted to give you those options because I've found that anything you can do to reduce travel in this profession—labor intensity—is always a good idea.

Now, what would constitute passive income for you under the narrow definition? (These might also be offerings on the left side of the accelerant curve.) My suggestions:

- Self-published hard copy books
- Ebooks
- Manuals (for example, *How to Do a Performance Evaluation*)
- Videos
- Podcasts
- Teleconference recordings available later
- Newsletter subscriptions
- Webinar recordings available later

- Recorded interviews
- Visuals (e.g., the process of innovation or decision making)[1]

For my expanded definition, in addition:

- One-on-one or group coaching
- Workshops and seminars
- Mastermind groups
- Livestreaming sessions with an audience

You have a great many options. My strong suggestion is that you should choose two or three (perhaps an ebook series on your value proposition, or a series of five-minute videos) and avoid being "scattered." Anything like a video or podcast can be turned into a series, with episodes appearing weekly or monthly. You can build a bank of these and simply release them on scheduled dates, thereby not having to be under the pressure of producing them on the spot. I've often combined subscriptions so that people have the choice of a newsletter, audio, and video for increasing fees.

You will build your brand through these offerings because people are entering the left side of your accelerant curve and will begin to move to the right (assuming you're creating such offerings), and you will become better known. Your referrals will increase.

Alanism
There's nothing at all wrong about repurposing your own IP on a regular basis in varied forms so that people have access to it in new ways.

The key to passive income on an advanced scale is an effective payment process that is a minimum of work for you. Many people use PayPal, but I'm not a big fan: not everyone uses it, and most people use standard credit cards to make purchases (and organizations certainly do). Therefore, you should establish a merchant account with your bank, which will take care of Mastercard, Visa, and Diners Club. (You have to set up American Express separately with the company itself, but it's quite simple.)

You should be using one bank for your business and personal accounts so that you're seen as a solid customer. The bank should be quite willing to set up your merchant account. That means that the money will be paid over the Internet and either directly deposited or come to you for processing. (I'll cover that in a minute.) You'll pay a transaction fee, usually under 3 percent. This is simply a cost of doing business.

As for the deposits, your software (such as 1ShoppingCart) can deposit orders directly into your bank account or forward them to you for processing. In the latter case you'll have a physical terminal for your desk and a virtual terminal for your computer. You can also process orders on an iPhone or iPad or other smart devices. My preference has always been to process orders myself because:

- I can accommodate discounts.
- Some people make errors in ordering.
- Refunds are sometimes necessary.
- I like to personally oversee my cash.
- I can question suspect orders.[2]

Obviously, these aren't issues to attend to in the first 90 days of your business, but they are something to consider as soon as the second year. You can repurpose your IP so that it becomes passive income content.

For example, I noted above that you can use teleconferences, webinars, and podcasts that you've created and delivered and recorded as products after the fact. You can put blog posts together by topic and appeal and create ebooks. There is nothing at all wrong with recycling your materials and offering them in different forms and configurations. In fact, it's the best way to raise additional income with the least labor.

I'm always reluctant to get too deep into technological alternatives with potentially brief life cycles in books with long shelf lives, but I do want to advise you to look into livestreaming your work at times. I currently offer two of these per month.

Livestreaming is the technology that allows people to watch you in real time, interact with questions via computers or phone lines, and also watch the recording on a delayed basis. To do this you can acquire a license for unlimited livestreaming on an annual basis from one of the companies providing these platforms. You'll need the right equipment to broadcast, but I suggest you simply hire a videographer who is expert in this technology. He or she might have a studio you can use, or you can rent a private room in a hotel if you don't have the space in your home.

You can have a live audience with you, which livens things up. My livestream sessions have people from all over the world (we'll discuss in the global market in the next segment) and all over the United States. I plan each one for 50–60 minutes, including questions, and I sell the entire series, not individual sessions. Someone joining "mid-season" receives all the previously recorded sessions.

This alternative obviously costs money—the license and the videographer—but you can easily make that back with an attractive profit once you build enough subscribers. You can repurpose material here *and* provide a brief promotional piece at the conclusion covering your upcoming events and offerings. I suggest you record a consistent opening and closing to the sessions.

Some of you will want to wait until you're more established to focus on passive income, and some of you will be eager to act immediately. There's no hurry, but there is strong potential whenever you are ready.

Working Globally

A major difference that's occurred in the 18 years since the first edition of this book, or even the 10 years since the last edition, is the vastly greater ability for solo consultants to work globally.

This is (largely) an English-speaking business world, the dollar remains the basis of worldwide currency, and American expertise is highly regarded in business. Combine that with technological advances, and global work is no longer something you aspire to do once your brand is strong.

You can do it now.

Digression

It's no accident that companies such as Apple, Amazon, Boeing, Microsoft, Uber, and the social media giants have grown up in America. This country's rather laissez faire attitude toward business has stimulated innovation and prudent risk taking. Overseas companies from Rolls Royce to Siemens view the United States as their primary market. The American companies named above all have vast international sales.

American expertise is highly regarded—global students fill our universities and business schools. And that expertise is what you're offering.

Here are six techniques to work overseas either in person or remotely. Many people in this profession have traveled the world, explored, taken family vacations, and generally improved the quality of their lives by creating international business and combining personal interests.

1. **Expand Your Base from Current, Multinational Clients**

   When you're doing business with domestic clients possessing international operations, try to meet the international executives (buyers). They're often at the US headquarters for meetings, or you can ask your current buyers for an email introduction. I've found that the work we do is culture independent and adaptable throughout a company's sites. Moreover, it's very advantageous for the entire company to experience the same processes and learning. Many overseas operations feel like poor cousins if they don't receive the same training and coaching being implemented in the United States.

2. **When You Travel, Inform Your Clients**

   You may be visiting other countries for a particular client or simply be on vacation. Let your existing multinational clients know and ask if you can be of service while you're traveling. A domestic buyer might well say, "Stop in while you're in town and visit Julia, our local general manager. Determine what she thinks the local market conditions will be next year. I'll let her know you're coming."

3. Write for Foreign Publications

There are business journals all over the world looking for content, and they are often very happy to have American experts provide that content. Simply Google business publications in India, or Germany, or South Africa and find out if they're publishing articles in English (or will translate them), if they accept articles from nonstaffers, and what the requirements are. This is easier than ever on the Internet with electronic publications.

4. Write for Domestic Publications Read Abroad

Harvard Business Review, Wall Street Journal, New York Times, and a wide variety of web-based business publications are read internationally. Submit articles to gain exposure to international (and, of course, domestic) readers. A good idea is to let a reporter know that you enjoyed his or her articles and would be pleased to be a source for future articles.

5. Offer to Speak

It's been said that an expert is someone with a briefcase over 50 miles from home. There are management associations all over the world—from Singapore to Dubai, from Buenos Aires to Cape Town—that love to add zest to their meetings with American speakers. You probably won't get paid or even have expenses reimbursed, but in conjunction with the techniques above, you have an excellent chance of appearing before scores, or even hundreds, of people who can purchase or recommend your services.

If you belong to international service clubs, such as Rotary, or an organization such as Toastmasters or the National Speakers

Association, you may find it easy not only to participate over-seas but also to have local people create introductions for you.

There is a direct relationship between distance and attraction. I live in Rhode Island, and if I tell people I'm coming to New York, it's no big deal. But if I tell them I'm coming to San Francisco, they'll definitely put time aside to talk to me. And if I tell them I'm coming to Hong Kong, they'll often host me and create activities around me.

6. Friends

You probably have friends or relationships or colleagues (school alumni are key here) who have settled overseas in permanent or temporary assignments. Get in touch with them. Ask about the local business climate and whether introductions would be something they would do for you. Let them know you're will-ing to come over if something can be set up. If possible, offer a quid pro quo (for example, maintaining contact with a child who's in college in the United States).

I wouldn't advise you to *begin* your career searching out overseas business, but I am trying to make you sensitive to the fact that when you're ready for it, it's not that difficult to pursue, and as an American abroad you'll often have an advantage you don't have in the competi-tive American marketplace. Don't discount the opportunities. I've seen consultants introduced by their buyer to the vice president for European operations at a dinner and then go back to their soup.

I introduced someone to a very influential person once, and he later said, "He wasn't interested in me." That wasn't quite true. My colleague didn't make himself interesting.

Alanism

The world is smaller than ever, so you can make a bigger splash than ever.

> **Chapter 9 Definitions**
>
> **S-curve theory:** The growth that we achieve should prompt us to leap to new growth opportunities when we have momentum, not when we've plateaued and are coasting.
>
> **Watertight doors:** The separate stages in our growth (survive, alive, arrive, thrive) that should be tightly sealed to prevent us from engaging in old, no longer appropriate habits and beliefs.
>
> **Passive income:** The narrow definition would include products and services sold with zero labor on your part. A broader definition would include services provided that allow you to be at home or close to home with minimal labor.

Notes

1. See my books *The Great Big Book of Process Visuals* (Las Brisas Research Press, 2000) and *The SECOND Great Big Book of Process Visuals* (Las Brisas Research Press, 2007) to see how these work and how they can be incorporated into a book for online sales.

2. A few times a year a credit card shows up with an address for the products to be sent to Russia, or Nigeria, or someplace that doesn't make sense, and it turns out the card number has been stolen.

Chapter

Living the Dream

The mark of truly successful people who are willing to take prudent risk to build their careers is that they prepare for setbacks and are resilient, *but that they also prepare for success*. It makes zero sense to go to the beach with board games, books, and iPads in case it rains but then neglect to bring your swim suit and snorkel in case the weather is great, as you'd hope it would be!

Building Your Brand

I've discussed the value of a strong brand, especially one built around your name, throughout the book, and even suggested that creating passive income early can assist in building your brand. Let's focus on the two major definitions of a *brand*, one academic and one pragmatic:

Academic. A brand is a uniform representation of quality. No one goes into a McDonald's, for example, to browse. They go in having already made the buying decision, based on an expectation of what to expect. Brands can be of high or low quality. One expects the best tailoring available in a Brioni suit and the best engineering possible in a Rolls Royce. And one would have expected a very average experience when flying the old USAir. Volkswagen has damaged its brand with its emissions scandal. After World War II Japanese brands were considered cheap, but they rose to represent very high quality and forged the second (now third at this writing) strongest economy in the world.

Pragmatic. A brand is how people think of you when you're not around. This business is often about timing. A client has a need, and you're available to fulfill the need. Or are you? If the client remembers you even though you're not in the office or on the schedule ("not around"), then that's a strong brand. But if the client has forgotten, or feels that you were simply as good as anyone else, then you're not likely to be asked if you're even remembered.

Alanism
Strong personal branding will lead to new and repeat business with virtually no cost of acquisition, meaning a brand is one of the most profitable benefits you can possibly create.

Right from the outset of your efforts as a consultant, I'd urge you to always consider building your brand. Many veterans in the profession have ignored this or failed to accomplish it, and have less profitable business and more labor in their work (because the client tells them how to consult, not trusting their expertise completely), and consequently less wealth (discretionary time).

Look at the "brand pyramid" in Figure 10.1, which shows the sequence of brand power. At the apex, the name itself has value (for example, "Get me McKinsey"). You can buy Ferrari watches today. Ferrari knows nothing about watchmaking, but its brand is so alluring that other companies pay just to be able to use it. In fact, most exotic carmakers sell a huge number of licensed items, from clothing to key chains.

Here are some simple and fast ways to begin building your brand today.

Attach Your Name to Everything Relevant

You don't want to be one of 10 excellent people whose names are in the hat when an excellent coach or strategy expert is sought. What you want is for the buyer to say, "Get me Gina for the strategy work."

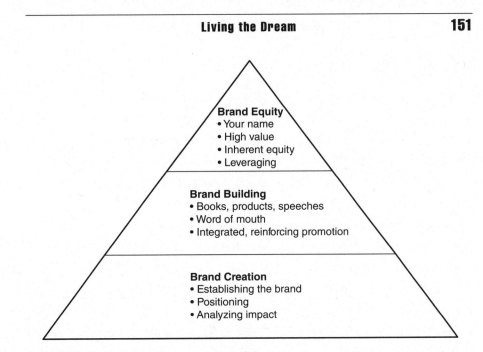

FIGURE 10.1: The brand pyramid.

Start attaching your name to your intellectual property. Don't produce "Ten Methods to Reduce Acquisition Costs"; make it "Tom Allen's Ten Methods...." If you write an ebook on coaching excellence don't use:

Coaching Excellence
By Norman Miller

Instead create:

Norman Miller's
Coaching Excellence

This may sound superficial and minor, but it's not. People remember techniques and insights that improve their work and their day, and they'll remember your name with it *if* you bother to include it and incorporate it.

If you have doubts about this, think about McKinsey, or Deloitte, or for that matter, Smuckers.

Associate Yourself with Strong Peers

There would be nothing wrong, as a consultant, with you saying something like this: "I agree with Alan Weiss that any type of hourly based fee is antithetical to a client's best interests." You don't have to have met me, and this isn't any kind of theft because you're providing attribution.

Establish who your peers are or who you aspire them to be and start mentioning their names and work—along with your own. If those other people's names are on buyer's minds, yours may be also. And here's a key hint: if you find yourself interviewing someone of stature whose brand is stronger than your own, never call it an "interview." Call it "a conversation with. . . ." That creates an equality instead of a subordinate/superior relationship. Don't merely ask questions and await the expert's answers; create a dialogue where you're also offering insights and value. Most people being interviewed prefer a natural conversation over rapid-fire questions in any case.

Stay in Touch Even When You're Out of Touch

Projects end, but relationships needn't. I'm not talking about newsletter lists and mass mailings (though they serve their purposes). I'm talking about private notes, even handwritten notes, to people who have helped you and can help you.

Find out something about your buyers' and recommenders' lives. Keep track of birthdays and anniversaries. Use social media, especially LinkedIn, to learn about promotions and transfers and new business ventures. Make note about family matters, such as personal hobbies or kids' accomplishments.

You don't have to do this often; you just have to do it about once a quarter. Don't rely on holiday cards; they tend to get lost in the pile. And express condolences when there's a reason to do so.

Maximize Your Unique Presence on the Internet

I have two blogs: one public (contrarianconsulting.com) and one private, for clients only (alanandthegang.com). I blog every single day on both, with rare exception, *even at this stage of my career*. And I try to make them unique: I have a weekly cartoon about my dogs, a monthly video, weekly podcasts, and so forth. I publish business insights as well as humor.

Many of us use videos that appear on our sites and on YouTube. You can create your own channels there for your own purposes. I strongly advise brief (less than two minute) videos to accommodate today's short attention spans that are professionally shot (you can do dozens at one sitting) and that you release your insights and techniques over time. Create a brief standard opening and closing. (You see a lot of these on LinkedIn, though they're too often too self-aggrandizing and too long.) Don't be derivative, as people are, for example, with the rapid-drawing technique, where someone creates a storyboard in speeded-up time.

Be provocative. Your opening should be, "I'm Suzy Sutton, and in the next two minutes you'll learn why strategy should be created in six hours and not six weeks." Wouldn't you be eager to hear the next two minutes?

Elevate Your Brand

Remember the S-curve phenomenon? Don't allow your brand to plateau or yourself to coast. Make the leap to the next S curve.

IBM began as International Business Machines, but always realized they were really in the information transmittal business, not the machine or punch-card business. Otherwise, they'd be out of business today. Instead, most of their profits come from consulting services.

Grow with the times and with your abilities and talents. Slam the watertight doors behind you and reach up. Move from inventory expert to operational excellence expert to business valuation expert. No one will do this for you, and don't merely depend on your marketplace.

Will Rogers said, "Even if you're on the right track, you'll still get run over if you just sit there."

Moving to Advisory (Vault) Work

Advisory work, in my intent here, is the help you provide a client through the insights, advice, and suggestions you provide. These may be proactive on your part or reactive, with you serving as a sounding board.

The normal payment mode for advisory work (these days often called "trusted advisor"—as if you could be an "untrusted advisor") is a retainer, which is an amount of money paid in a lump sum at one time or periodically. The retainer is the payment method, not the actual form of work. As I pointed out earlier, it is different from the retainer paid an attorney, *which is merely a deposit against which the attorney deducts his or her hourly fees.*

Since advisory work does not require you to complete a project, or even to be on the client's site, it is the lowest labor relationship you can achieve along with the highest pay, since it's very valuable, lucrative work. This is why I consider it a vault item on the accelerant curve and why it's possible to move to high fee and low labor concurrently, even though many people see that as a paradox.

Advisory work is a vault item in a generic sense, in that many people can provide the service, but it's also highly unique *in that no two of us will do it in the same way with exactly the same skills.*

Let's take a look at the positioning required to be a trusted advisor, which you can see in Figure 10.2.

When neither respect nor affection exists, you're merely a vendor. You might as well be selling office plants, computers, or paving services. You would be selected by procurement based on low price. Enough said.

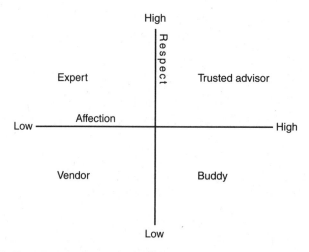

FIGURE 10.2:   Respect versus affection.

When you have high affection—the buyer really likes you—but low respect, you're a buddy. You might be hired for some low-level, low-impact assignments and would probably be delegated down to HR and other minor functions in the organization.

If you achieve high respect but low affection, you're an expert. You might be asked to complete a forensic financial assignment or analyze sales expenses, or create assessment tests. You are valuable within a limited dimension. (Picture the courtroom expert witness.)

However, when you are both respected and liked, tempering the former with the reality of the latter so that advice is perceived as honest and objective, you can achieve trusted advisor status. And that means that you'll be on a retainer basis to be available.

Advisory fees vary *and are not based on conceptual agreement.* There is no project here requiring objectives, metrics, and value. There is merely access to you when needed. But let's review the three options for you to offer in considering what fee to charge:

> **Alanism**
>
> The retainer paid to maintain you as a trusted advisor is actually paid to gain access to your "smarts" on an as-needed basis.

1. *Numbers.* Who is entitled to contact you? Is it solely the buyer, or also the buyer's two or three top lieutenants? (Advisory work in one company is difficult with more than just a few top people in any given unit.)

2. *Scope.* Are you available during your business hours (for example, East Coast, United States) or the client's business hours (for example, the West Coast of the United States or Germany)? Will you appear on site if needed to discuss issues in person? What is your response time to calls and emails?

3. *Duration.* How long will the relationship last?

Based on these variables, you establish your fee. I recommend that for executives in large organizations, depending on these variables, your fee should be at least $7,500 to $10,000 per month. *You need to create at least a three-month minimum, because less time doesn't provide enough opportunity for the advisory role to be fully utilized.*

You should be paid at the beginning of that three-month period, not monthly, and the contract should be noncancelable for any reason. This isn't an issue of how often the client uses your help; it's an issue of how valuable your help is on the occasions it is sought. Your client doesn't need instant access but rather *responsiveness*. My guarantees, as noted above, have been to return calls within 90 minutes and email within a half day during my normal business hours (where I reside) and I usually beat that.

Never feel that if you're not frequently contacted that you're not providing value. The value of your being there when needed and responding promptly with critical advice is your value. Here's a discussion I had with one of my coaching clients I'll call "Rich":

> **Rich:** My client (who's an advisory client) told me that he barely used me this past year, so he's thinking of either reducing the fee or discontinuing for a while. What should I say to him?
>
> **Me:** Did your client have a fire this past year?
>
> **Rich:** No, why?
>
> **Me:** Did he cancel his fire insurance?

Our value is in our potential to help. It's not unusual to have retainers of six or 12 months, or even those that renew annually. I was on retainer to Calgon for five years when it was in the water-treatment business. I also had, concurrently, traditional projects with them in several areas. But the CEO kept me on personal retainer. At the time the fee was $120,000 ($10,000 per month), but if I was paid at the outset, it was reduced to $100,000, which I would receive promptly on January 2.

In November of the third year on this arrangement, I went to see the CEO to renew it for the next year.

"No, not the same way," he said. I was flummoxed. What had I done wrong to end the agreement?

"You've been more valuable than I had anticipated, and I want to make it $130,000 from this point on."

That was only the second time in my life I had been speechless.[1]

For smaller businesses your fee might be in the range of $5,000 to $7,500 per month. It will take some more work to convince these business owners of the value of your "insurance" and not allow them to also use you on site for project work without additional payments.

It's not too soon for you to begin thinking of what your life might be like with a dozen of such advisory clients in your stable.

Remember that no one will know that you offer such services *unless you tell them*. Use war stories (as I've just written here) and examples. Suggest advisory work as option 3 in your proposals (Chapter 7) and/ or as follow-on work to successfully completed projects. It's common for happy clients to want to keep you around after such success, but they often have to be educated on how to do that because they assume you don't have anything else to offer!

There are many consultants in my community doing exclusively advisory work. There are others who augment their careers nicely with it, because they also love project work.

One final word: I'm writing this from our August vacation spot on Nantucket, where I routinely take calls on the beach from clients all over the world, requiring less than an hour a day in total. My wife asks me early during our stay when she joins me on the beach, "Have you paid for our vacation yet?"

Intellectual Property and Thought Leadership

Intellectual property (IP) consists of those ideas, statements, models, visuals, and so forth that are uniquely yours. That doesn't mean *every* word and line has to be uniquely yours (pretty much impossible), but rather that the relationships and models you create are yours.

Figure 10.3 illustrates an example of IP.

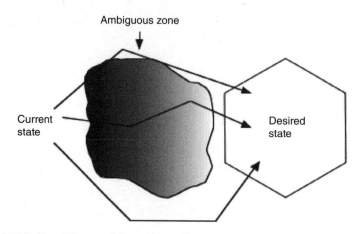

FIGURE 10.3: The ambiguous zone.

You can see that the words, shapes, and lines are not unique. But my model depicting the fact that people are clear on the new, desired state, but often uncertain about how to transit to that point (hence, needing leadership during the journey), is unique.

Here's another (text) example: "I urge you to follow the 'oxygen mask rule': They tell you on planes to place your own mask on first before helping others, and you need to do the same in your career. You can't help others until you've helped yourself."

Or this: "My 'lobster principle' is that a lobster has to shed its external skeleton—its shell—and become vulnerable in order to grow. People also have to allow vulnerability if they are to grow."

It's that simple. Whether visual, textual, or auditory, your IP helps distinguish you mightily in the marketplace. Ideally, it should be related to your value proposition and your branding efforts, and you should be creating it *weekly* and disseminating it through your blog, newsletter, articles, speeches, conversation, videos, and so forth.

Here are some others readily found in such sources:

"What got you here won't get you there."—Marshall Goldsmith

The black swan phenomenon described by Nassim Taleb.

Walt Mossberg, the technology columnist and consult-ant, pointing out that we don't talk about "plugging into the electrical grid" when we use a toaster, so why do we talk about "going onto the Internet"?

You develop IP by considering what you're trying to do to improve the client's condition and then depicting it in a variety of useful ways. Just as different musical pieces may use the same notes but still be distinct, you can use the same words in differing contexts.[2]

When you are producing such IP on a regular basis and disseminating it widely you can aspire to *thought leadership* in your field. While this is an increasingly overused phrase these days, it stands for something basically important: some people are recognized as the leading thinkers (providers of IP) in their chosen fields.

Some examples, at least at this writing:

1. Executive coaching: Marshall Goldsmith
2. Creative thinking: Seth Godin
3. Personal development: Marcus Buckingham
4. Positive psychology: Martin Seligman
5. Influence and persuasion: Robert Cialdini, Jonah Berger
6. Social and interpersonal dynamics: Malcolm Gladwell, Dan Pink
7. Solo consulting and entrepreneurialism: Alan Weiss

You may have other candidates or disagree with my list. But my point is that if you're in these fields—or even interested in them—you *must* know who these people are. Someone may not agree with me in terms of my approaches to solo consulting, but if you're in the field and don't know who I am, then you're simply an amateur who isn't trying very hard.

What does this mean for business? Well, for a long time (and even now, for many), McKinsey & Company was considered a thought leader in corporate strategy. That means that many a CEO picked up the phone and said, "Get me McKinsey," without seeking any other source, confident that the board would support the choice and a great job would be done.

That's rather invaluable, wouldn't you say?

I've saved this particular discussion of IP for the latter part of the book because it's something that's needed when you're getting started *and forever thereafter*. You might as well get in the habit now. I'm still doing this on nearly a daily basis. If you review the 20 or so figures in these chapters you see IP. If you compare these to the last edition in 2009 and the first edition in 2000, you'll find a few the same, some different, and some new.

Alanism

I helped dramatically accelerate a woman's entire career when I suggested she stop calling herself "a thought leader" and begin calling herself "*The* thought leader."

That's because your and my thinking enlarges and grows as we gain experience and knowledge. Thus, IP isn't a laborious, desperate search for new ideas hunched over a workbench late at night with a glass of scotch. It's rather a spontaneous creation of new ideas and new configurations. (The glass of scotch is optional.)

What does this mean?

It means that to grow your business and achieve the thrive level on the progression through the watertight doors (itself thought leadership IP) you have to constantly capture the ideas, insights, and initiatives you develop deliberately or accidentally during the day. It's that simple—in that you're creating such IP as you go about your normal pursuits—and that difficult—in that you must *capture* them.

A lot of our best ideas are evanescent, disappearing as soon as they appear. We need to codify them.

Here's what you have to do. It's what I do:

- Have a pad or recording device (iPhones are great) always nearby. When you have a good idea, record it or make a quick note or sketch.

- When you're engaged in a meeting with a client or colleagues— or your attorney or accountant or whomever—make a note of something that comes up *that you think may be useful in other contexts*. Here's an example I use: it's insufficient to have receivables if they're not received, which is why being paid in advance is so important—you never have to worry about being paid once you begin a project.

- If the IP is still attractive to you the next morning, then try using it. If it isn't—or you can't even remember why you wrote it down—simply discard it.

- For the IP you decide to keep and use, begin to experiment with it *immediately* in your writing, speaking, and conversations.

- Catalog your IP so those items you don't use frequently, but which are nonetheless powerful, are not forgotten. You need to be able to recall text and visuals by topic and context. A spreadsheet or a simple data file app will take care of this nicely.

Someone said, "You are what you eat." In consulting, you are what you create.

The Essence of a Career

If you've ever gone to the Academy in Firenze to see the statue of David, you have experienced the awe involved in viewing this magnificent work of art, even though you may have seen photos and thought you were prepared for it. Michelangelo carved it out of a single piece of discarded marble.[3]

The perhaps apocryphal story is that Michelangelo was asked how he managed to carve it. He replied, "I simply carved away anything that didn't look like David."

Your career comprises two elements on the "thrive" level (Figure 9.2):

1. What you are passionate about doing.
2. What you are excellent at doing.

Carve away everything else and you'll have a career that is a work of art.

Figure 10.4 shows another way to view these factors.

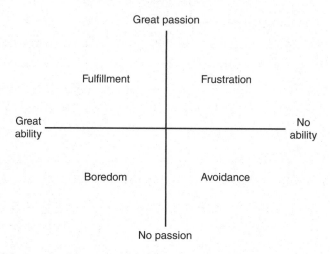

FIGURE 10.4: Passion and ability.

In the bottom left you see a great many corporate jobs, where someone has great talents but no passion for the work, and in the upper right you see the frustrated entrepreneurs who are passionate about something for which they have little or no talent.

Too many consultants, as they become successful, continue to chase money and take on difficult, labor-intensive, and uninteresting work. (They haven't sealed the watertight doors.) Hence, they don't grow, but plateau.

It's never too soon to begin your focus on your passion and start getting great at it. Those people I mentioned earlier at the top of their fields are people doing what they love and doing it excellently. This achieves the perfect synergy between career and life.

You'll do a great deal while you're learning the business, some of which will stand you in good stead forever, and some of which you can abandon and forget. What I've come to call the "Michelangelo principle" is that, counterintuitively perhaps, you should carve away what doesn't seem appropriate for your career, but never try to add on other pieces just because other people are using them. Imagine

Alanism
Never use other people's metrics to assess your own success. Create your own.

what David would have looked like with patches of marble added here and there? The story is ben trovato: If it isn't true, it should be!

I'm not precluding growth, of course, but I am admonishing you to set your own course. Don't try to be me (or anyone else) in this profession; simply try to learn from us and emulate successful behaviors and habits. But adjust them to your own proclivities, your own passions, your own strengths.

I was frustrated by cross-country skiing, because you merely followed in the ruts of other skiers or the ruts that some machine created for the lodge. If you found yourself behind slow people, you had to pass them using other ruts or create your own until you returned to the original ruts. (I can't call them "trails": they were merely ruts in the snow!)

I found this hugely boring.

By contrast, there was far more risk in downhill skiing, but far more excitement. There was the danger of a fall, but we all quickly recovered from falls and crashes so long as we were acting safely and not imprudently. We were able to gather speed and try tougher (and more thrilling) hills.

This is living!

I always felt more deserving at the lodge at the end of the day with a drink after downhill skiing—taking some risks, braving the fears, and being exhilarated by the ride—rather than having traveled in ruts. That's how I've always felt about my career.

Digression

Someone tried to goad me once by saying at an event: "You've only had one really good idea in your life, and you've merely recycled it and repurposed it endlessly."

"Yeah," I replied, "isn't that great?!!"

Consulting is a career, not a job, not "work." It's the intent to improve the condition of your buyer and your buyer's operation. You are offering value, not selling services. *You are an asset and a partner, not a vendor.*

FIGURE 10.5: The effect of mindset on success.

Remember that you cannot position yourself or be perceived as another priority on the buyer's metaphorical plate. You are the *solution* that resolves all those other priorities. You are a unique asset, not a commodity. Hence, you are paid by value, not by time. You are not hired—you form a partnership.

I think you've realized by now that your mindset will control your success. The sequence looks like the one shown in Figure 10.5).

What you believe about yourself will create attitudes, which are manifested in behaviors. This is purely internal control, if you allow it to be. It's important to know who you are and what you're trying to accomplish. (When I ask most coaching clients, "Who do you want to be next year?" they respond with *what they want to be doing*, which is the answer to a very different kind of question.) You need to believe that you are an expert, with the skills, talents, and abilities necessary to help any client who wants to be helped. Your attitude must be that you are smart enough and skilled enough to attract clients, deliver great work, and expand business. This will be expressed in behaviors that include confidence, assertiveness, persuasiveness, humor, perspective, and resilience.

Getting started in consulting is really about getting started in your own mind.

The first sale is to yourself.

Chapter 10 Definitions

Brand: A uniform representation of quality (good or poor) and the way people tend to think of you when you're not around (if they think of you).

Thought leadership: Providing the seminal or provocative ideas in a given field that encourages other to improve, and for which the creator is cited and acknowledged.

Notes

1. This executive would call me on Monday nights before Tuesday morning board meetings to review his presentation. He would call during halftime of *Monday Night Football*, not because he liked football, but because he knew that I did.

2. But if you're ever unsure if something is yours or someone else's, *always* provide attribution. This is not only ethical, it will place you in a far better light than suggesting that something that may not be yours is your own.

3. The statue was once in the main square, but was considered so valuable and rare that no less than Donatello created a duplicate to be displayed outside in the early fifteenth century so that the original could be protected inside.

The End

101 Questions for Any Sales Situation You'll Ever Face

This material is intended to provide questions to ask in virtually any sales situation, thereby accomplishing the following five goals:

1. Maintaining a conversational and nonsales approach.
2. Keeping the other party talking in order to learn.
3. Avoiding deselection by volunteering very little yourself.
4. Finding the buyer, building a relationship, and closing business.
5. Accelerating the entire sales process.

I strongly advise that you personalize the generic questions so that they support your particular practice or business.

You might choose to take these questions on calls, to keep them by the phone, or to use them as the basis for printing out your own questions to keep in your briefcase or calendar.

The questions are deliberately overlapping and stop just short of being duplicative. Essentially, you want to elicit the same information in as many diverse ways as possible.

A Few Guidelines for Use

- Don't interrogate people. It's seldom necessary to ask even the majority of questions in any one category.

- Employ follow-up questions. The questions contained herein are triggers that may engender a response that demands further clarification.

- Trust is essential for candor. The other party will be most honest and responsive when trust is established (that is, they believe you have their best interests in mind).

- Never be content with a single question, no matter how satisfying the answer appears to be. Some people will attempt to deceive you to save their ego, and others will inadvertently deceive you because they misunderstood the question. I recommend that you use at least three questions per category if the answers are consistent, and six or more if the answers appear to be inconsistent.

These questions are rational, objective, and most of all, based on common sense and simple discourse. Try not to be distracted or to digress yourself until the answer you're seeking in any given category is forthcoming. For example, it's dysfunctional to ask questions about objectives if you haven't asked the questions to satisfy you that you're talking to an economic buyer. Discipline is best.

Ironically, the longer you take to find the right answers, the more you accelerate the business.

Qualifying the Prospect

This is the process of determining whether the inquiry is appropriate for your business in terms of size, relevance, seriousness, and related factors. In other words, you don't want to pursue a lead that can't result in legitimate—and worthwhile—business.

Questions

1. Why do you think we might be a good match?
2. Is there budget allocated for this project?
3. How important is this need (on a scale of 1 to 10)?
4. What is your timing to accomplish this?
5. Who, if anyone, is demanding that this be accomplished?
6. How soon are you willing to begin?
7. Have you made a commitment to proceed, or are you still analyzing?
8. What are your key decision criteria in choosing a resource?
9. Have you tried this before (will this be a continuing endeavor)?
10. Is your organization seeking formal proposals for this work?

Key Point: You want to determine whether the potential work is large enough for your involvement, relevant to your expertise, and near enough on the horizon to merit rapid responsiveness.

Finding the Economic Buyer

The economic buyer is the person who can write a check in return for your value contribution. He or she is the *only* buyer to be concerned about. Contrary to a great deal of poor advice, the economic buyer is virtually *never* in human resources, training, meeting planning, or related support areas.

Questions

11. Whose budget will support this initiative?
12. Who can immediately approve this project?
13. To whom will people look for support, approval, and credibility?

14. Who controls the resources required to make this happen?

15. Who has initiated this request?

16. Who will claim responsibility for the results?

17. Who will be seen as the main sponsor and/or champion?

18. Do you have to seek anyone else's approval?

19. Who will accept or reject proposals?

20. If you and I were to shake hands, could I begin tomorrow?

Key Point: The larger the organization, the more the number of economic buyers. They need not be the CEO or owner, but they must be able to authorize and produce payment. Committees are never economic buyers.

Rebutting Objections

"Obstacles are those terrible things you see when you take your eyes off the goal," said philosopher Hannah Arendt. Objections are a sign of *interest*. Turn them around to your benefit. Once you demolish objections, there is no longer a reason not to proceed in a partnership.

Questions (in responding to an economic buyer's objections)

21. Why do you feel that way? (Get at the true cause.)

22. If we resolve this, can we then proceed? (Is this the sole objection?)

23. But isn't that exactly why you need me? (The reversal approach.)

24. What would satisfy you? (Make the buyer answer the objection.)

25. What can we do to overcome that? (Demonstrate joint accountability.)

26. Is this unique? (Is there precedent for overcoming it?)

27. What's the consequence? (Is it really serious or merely an annoyance?)

28. Isn't that low probability? (Worry about likelihoods, not the remote.)

29. Shall I address that in the proposal? (Let's focus on value.)

30. Why does it even matter in light of the results? (The ROI is the point.)

Key Points: Don't be on the defensive by trying to slay each objection with your sword, or you'll eventually fall on it. Embrace the buyer in the solutions and demonstrate that some objections are insignificant when compared with benefits (for example, there will always be some unhappy employees in any change effort).

Establishing Objectives

Objectives are the *outcomes* that represent the client's desired and improved conditions. They are never inputs (for example, reports, focus groups, manuals) but rather always outputs (for example, increased sales, reduced attrition, improved teamwork). Clear objectives prevent scope creep and enable a rational engagement and disengagement to take place, resulting in much greater consulting efficiency and profit margins. (Note that the fourth, fifth, and sixth items here—objectives, measures, and value—are the basis of conceptual agreement.)

Questions

31. What is the ideal outcome you'd like to experience?

32. What results are you trying to accomplish?

33. What better product/service/customer condition are you seeking?

34. Why are you seeking to do this (work/project/engagement)?

35. How would the operation be different as a result of this work?

36. What would be the return on investment (sales, assets, equity, and the like)?

37. How would image/repute/credibility be improved?

38. What harm (for example, stress, dysfunction, turf wars, and so forth) would be alleviated?

39. How much would you gain on the competition as a result?

40. How would your value proposition be improved?

Key Points: Most buyers know what they want *but not necessarily what they* need. *By pushing the buyer on the end results you are helping to articulate and formalize the client's perceived benefits, thereby increasing your own value in the process. Without clear objectives you do not have a legitimate project.*

Establishing Metrics

Metrics are measures of progress toward the objectives that enable you and the client to ascertain the rate and totality of success. They assign proper credit to you and your efforts and also signify when the project is complete (objectives are met) and it is proper to disengage.

Questions

41. How will you know we've accomplished your intent?

42. How, specifically, will the operation be different when we're done?

43. How will you measure this?

44. What indicators will you use to assess our progress?

45. Who or what will report on our results (against the objectives)?

46. Do you already have measures in place you intend to apply?

47. What is the rate of return (on sales, investment, and the like) that you seek?

48. How will we know the public, employees, and/or customers perceive it?

49. Each time we talk, what standard will tell us we're progressing?

50. How would you know it if you tripped over it?

Key Points: Measures can be subjective, so long as you and the client agree on who is doing the measuring and how. For example, the buyer's observation that he or she is called upon less to settle turf disputes and has fewer complaints from direct reports aimed at colleagues are valid measures for the objective of improved teamwork.

Assessing Value

Determining the value of the project for the client's organization is *the* most critical aspect of conceptual agreement and preproposal interaction. That's because when the buyer stipulates to significant value, the fee is placed in proper perspective (ROI) and is seldom an issue of contention. Conversations with the buyer should always focus on value and never on fee or price.

Questions

51. What will these results mean for your organization?

52. How would you assess the actual return (ROI, ROA, ROS, ROE, and the like)?

53. What would be the extent of the improvement (or correction)?

54. How will these results impact the bottom line?

55. What are the *annualized* savings (first year might be deceptive)?

56. What is the intangible impact (for example, on repute, safety, comfort, and so forth)?

57. How would you, personally, be better off or better supported?

58. What is the scope of the impact (on customers, employees, vendors)?

59. How important is this compared to your overall responsibilities?

60. What if this fails?

Key Point: Subjective value (stress alleviated) can be every bit as important as more tangible results (higher sales). Never settle for "Don't worry, it's important." Find out how important, because that will dictate the acceptable fee range.

Determining the Budget Range

Too much guessing takes place in the absence of a general understanding about how much the prospect intends to invest (prior to understanding the full value proposition). In many cases, the budget is fixed and entirely inappropriate, and in others it represents a better understanding of the ROI than that of the consultant! (Don't forget, this presupposes you're talking to an economic buyer.)

Questions

61. Have you arrived at a budget or investment range for this project?
62. Are funds allocated, or must they be requested?
63. What is your expectation of investment required?
64. So we don't waste time, are there parameters to remain within?
65. Have you done this before, and at what investment level?
66. What are you able to authorize during this fiscal year?
67. Can I assume that a strong proposition will justify proper expenditure?
68. How much are you prepared to invest to gain these dramatic results?
69. For a dramatic return, will you consider a larger investment?
70. Let's be frank: What are you willing to spend?

Key Points: There is nothing wrong with exceeding the budget expectation if you muster a strong enough value proposition. But don't even proceed with a proposal if the prospect has a seriously misguided expectation of the investment need or simply has an inadequate, fixed budget.

Preventing Unforeseen Obstacles

As comedienne Gilda Radner used to say, "It's always something." Inevitably, it seems, the best-laid plains are undermined by objections, occurrences, and serendipity from left field. Fortunately, there are questions to establish some preventive actions against even the unforeseen.

Questions

71. Is there anything we haven't discussed that could get in the way?

72. In the past, what has occurred to derail potential projects like this?

73. What haven't I asked you that I should have about the environment?

74. What do you estimate the probability is of our going forward?

75. Are you surprised by anything I've said or that we've agreed upon?

76. At this point, are you still going to make this decision yourself?

77. What, if anything, do you additionally need to hear from me?

78. Is anything likely to change in the organization in the near future?

79. Are you awaiting the results of any other initiatives or decisions?

80. If I get this proposal to you tomorrow, how soon will you decide?

Key Points: Make sure that your project isn't contingent upon other events transpiring (or not transpiring). If the buyer is holding out on you, these questions will make it more difficult to dissemble. Build into your proposal benefits to outweigh the effects of any external factors.

Increasing the Size of the Sale

Once conceptual agreement is gained, it makes sense to capitalize on the common ground and strive for the largest possible relationship. Most consultants don't obtain larger contracts *because they don't ask for or suggest them.* You can't possibly lose anything attempting to increase the business at this juncture.

Questions

81. Would you be amenable to my providing a variety of options?

82. Is this the only place (division, department, geography) applicable?

83. Would it be wise to extend this through implementation and oversight?

84. Should we plan to also coach key individuals essential to the project?

85. Would you benefit from benchmarking against other firms?

86. Would you also like an idea of what a retainer might look like?

87. Are there others in your position with like needs I should see?

88. Do your subordinates possess the skills to support you appropriately?

89. Should we run focus groups/other sampling to test employee reactions?

90. Would you like me to test customer response at various stages?

Key Points: If you don't ask, you don't get. Don't throw everything including the kitchen sink into your proposal in an attempt to justify your fee. Instead, unbundle what you're capable of providing and add them back in at additional fee.

Going for the Close

Homestretch, but not across the finish line. Runners who slow up at the approaching tape lose to someone else with a better late kick. Run through the tape at full speed by driving the conversation right through the close of the sale and the check clearing the bank.

Questions

91. If the proposal reflects our last discussions, how soon can we begin?

92. Is it better to start immediately or wait for the first of the month?

93. Is there anything at all preventing our working together at this point?

94. How rapidly are you prepared to begin once you see the proposal?

95. If you get the proposal tomorrow, can I call Friday at 10 for approval?

96. While I'm here, should I begin some of the preliminary work today?

97. Would you like to shake hands and get started, proposal to follow?

98. Do you prefer writing a corporate check or wiring the funds electronically?

99. May I allocate two days early next week to start my interviews?

100. Can we proceed?

Key Points: There is never *a better time than when you're in front of the buyer and he or she is in agreement and excited about the project. Even without a proposal, beginning immediately pours cement on the conceptual agreement and greatly diminishes the possibility of being derailed by surprise.*

The Most Vital Question

All of the preceding 100 questions are actually based on the reaction to one question, which we often fail to ask of the most difficult person of all. And unlike most of the prior inquiries, it's a simple binary question, with a clear yes-or-no response.

Question

101. Do you believe it yourself?

Key Point: The first sale is always to yourself.

Suggested Reading in the Field

'm limiting this to the four books of mine I think are must reads for new people (in addition to this one) and including others I admire:

Million Dollar Consulting, 5th ed. (McGraw-Hill, 2017)

Value-Based Fees, 2nd ed. (Pfeiffer, 2008)

Million Dollar Consulting® Proposals (John Wiley & Sons, 2011)

Million Dollar Maverick (Bibliomotion, 2016)

The Consultant's Calling (Geoffrey Bellman: Jossey-Bass, 2002)

The Capitalist Philosophers (Andrea Gabor: Three Rivers Press, 2000)

The Effective Executive (Peter Drucker: HarperCollins, 2006)

Managing in Turbulent Times (Peter Drucker: HarperBusiness, 1993)

Flawless Consulting (Peter Block: Pfeiffer, 2011)

Learned Optimism (Martin Seligman: Vintage Books, 2006)

Contagious (Jonah Berger: Simon & Schuster, 2016)

Invisible Influence (Jonah Berger: Simon & Schuster, 2017)

Influence (Robert Cialdini: William Morrow, 1993)

To Sell Is Human (Daniel Pink: Riverhead Books, 2012)

Antifragile (Nassim Taleb: Random House, 2014)

What Got You Here Won't Get You There (Marshall Goldsmith: Hyperion, 2007)

Sample Proposal

Situation

Since becoming executive vice president for XXXXXXXX four months ago, you have discovered numerous strengths in the organization as well as critical barriers to success. These qualities are even more significant given the goal to grow the business at a rate significantly above the historical. While doing so, you are expected to maintain the culture of the organization that is deemed valuable and productive by both your superiors and subordinates.

Your success depends upon the creation and successful implementation of a powerful strategy through an organization with the right people in the right roles acting in concert with one another. Past success in building successful relationships with clients and peers will serve you well. However, in this role, you must manage a larger and more diverse organization than before. Further, you have a finite amount of time to demonstrate that you are the right person to lead the organization at this time.

Objectives

1. Provide a professional, external sounding board for you.

2. Develop and implement an integration process to accelerate your success as the executive vice president.

3. Provide a professional, expert view of the talent at the top of the organization.

4. Develop a clear, compelling strategy.

5. Develop and use a simple, though powerful, implementation plan.

6. Increase cooperation and collaboration among the top leaders to ensure attainment of the goals. Specifically, reduce the friction between two of the executive committee members, whose talents are each needed to achieve success.

Measures of Success

1. Agreement between XXXXXXXX and yourself regarding the specific outcomes for which you are accountable.

2. Reduced time to make, and increased confidence in, decisions.

3. Increase in revenue while maintaining profit margin.

4. Evidence that the strategy and goals are clear and that behaviors are aligned in support of the plans. Such evidence will include:

   a. Spontaneous conversations that indicate such

   b. Increased cooperation

   c. Increase in the number of ideas that come from the lower levels of the organization to the top

5. Decrease in the number of conversations needed to manage the conflict at the top.

6. Positive feedback from the chief operating officer regarding your performance for both financial management and leadership.

Value

- Increase in sales of $1.5 million over the past year will add $300,000 to net profit, taking the total net profit to $1.3 million.

- Decrease in conflict at the top level will reduce time spent in conversation with those involved.

- Decrease in time to market of new ideas or approaches.

- Acceleration of your ability to make positive impact.

- Create a useful framework for decision making, reducing time to do so.

Method and Options

Option 1

For a period of six months, conduct face-to-face meetings with you as needed and provide unlimited telephone consultation.

Meet with each of your direct reports to more fully understand them and the organizational context.

Conduct a meeting of the direct-report team to debrief observations and further accelerate your integration.

Meet with the executive committee to ensure clarity of purpose and goals and alignment. Create a strategic framework to ensure the attainment of growth and profitability goals.

Meet with you and XXXXXXXX to resolve the issues between them and among the three of you.

Meet with you and XXXXXXXX to establish goals and expectations, and to achieve alignment and support for your plans.

Option 2

All the elements of option 1, plus:

A follow-up meeting of the direct-report group at the five-month mark to identify new opportunities, challenges, and ideas, and to solidify your leadership.

Option 3

All the elements of options 1 and 2, and:

Survey the entire organization to more thoroughly understand the context and any cultural barriers to the effective implementation of your strategy. Analysis and debrief of results with the direct-report team included.

Timing

The initial interviews and meetings will be completed within eight weeks of the commencement of this project.

The consultation with you and the executive committee will continue for a total of six months.

Joint Accountabilities

XXXXXXXX will provide Constance Dierickx, PhD, as the project leader. She will be continually involved in all aspects of the project and will serve as the primary contact with XXXXXXXX. We will sign non-disclosure agreements as requested, and all work contents remain the property of XXXXXXXX.

XXXXXXXX will provide us with reasonable access to key management people, documentation, and company information, as appropriate, within the time frames outlined above. XXXXXXXX will be responsible for scheduling of meetings and for obtaining necessary facilities, equipment, and related support for meetings. XXXXXXXX agrees to the fee structure outlined below and will adhere to the reimbursement of expenses procedures as specified.

Terms and Conditions

Option 1:	$60,000
Option 2:	$70,000
Option 3:	$85,000

Payment terms are one-half fee due upon the signing of this letter of agreement and one-half due 45 days hence.

Reasonable travel and living expenses will be submitted monthly as accrued, at cost, and payment is due upon receipt of the invoice.

This project is noncancelable, and agree-upon payment terms are due as described. You may postpone or delay any part of the work as you deem necessary. The quality of our work is guaranteed. If we do not meet your objectives, as stated above, we will refund your fee.

Acceptance

Your selection of options below and your signature—or alternatively, your deposit or full payment—indicate acceptance of all terms and conditions herein.

_____ Option 1 _____ Option 2 _____ Option 3

We are submitting our deposit in the amount of $_____ or our full payment with our 10 percent discount in the amount of $_____.

_____   _____
John Adams   Alan Weiss
President   President
Acme Co.   Summit   Consulting
                                    Group, Inc.

Date:_____   Date:_____

Sample Long Biographical Sketch

Alan Weiss: Biographical Sketch

Alan Weiss is one of those rare people who can say he is a consultant, speaker, and author and mean it. His consulting firm, Summit Consulting Group, Inc., has attracted clients such as Merck, Hewlett-Packard, GE, Mercedes-Benz, State Street Corporation, the Times Mirror Company, the Federal Reserve, the New York Times Company, Toyota, and over 200 other leading organizations. He has served on the boards of directors of the Trinity Repertory Company, a Tony Award–winning New England regional theater, and of Festival Ballet Providence, and has chaired the Newport International Film Festival.

His speaking typically includes 20 keynotes a year at major conferences, and he has been a visiting faculty member at Case Western Reserve University, Boston College, Tufts, St. John's University, the University of Illinois, the Institute of Management Studies, and the University of Georgia's Terry College of Business. He has held an appointment as adjunct professor in the College of Business at the

University of Rhode Island, where he taught courses on advanced management and consulting skills. He holds the record for selling out the highest-priced workshop at the time (on entrepreneurialism) in the (then) 21-year history of New York City's Learning Annex. His PhD is in psychology. He has served on the board of governors of Harvard University's Center for Mental Health and the Media.

He is an inductee into the Professional Speaking Hall of Fame and the concurrent recipient of the National Speakers Association Council of Peers Award of Excellence, representing the top 1 percent of professional speakers in the world. He has also been named a Fellow of the Institute of Management Consultants, one of only two people in the world holding both those designations.

His prolific publishing includes over 500 articles and 60 books, including his best seller, *Million Dollar Consulting* (from McGraw-Hill). His newest is *Threescore and More* (Taylor and Francis). His books have been on the curricula at Villanova, Temple University, UC Berkeley, and the Wharton School of Business, and have been translated into 15 languages.

He is interviewed and quoted frequently in the media. His career has taken him to 60 countries and 49 states. (He is afraid to go to North Dakota.) *Success* magazine has cited him in an editorial devoted to his work as "a worldwide expert in executive education." The *New York Post* called him "one of the most highly regarded independent consultants in America." He is the winner of the prestigious Axiem Award for Excellence in Audio Presentation.

He is the recipient of the Lifetime Achievement Award of the American Press Institute, the first ever for a nonjournalist, and one of only seven awarded in the 65-year history of the association. His annual Thought Leadership Conference draws world famous experts as speakers. In 2017, his featured speaker was Harvard Distinguished Professor Dan Gilbert, whose work on happiness has drawn over 15 million TED views.

He has coached former Miss Rhode Island and Miss America candidates in interviewing skills. He once appeared on the popular

American TV game show *Jeopardy!*, where he lost badly in the first round to a dancing waiter from Iowa.

Alan has been married to the lovely Maria for 50 years, and they have two children and twin granddaughters. They reside in East Greenwich, Rhode Island, with their dogs: Bentley, a white German shepherd, and Coco.

Sample Short Biographical Sketch

Alan Weiss is the only nonjournalist in history to receive the Lifetime Achievement Award from the American Press Institute. He has authored 64 books, which appear in 12 languages. His clients have included Mercedes-Benz, Merck, Hewlett-Packard, the New York Times Company, and over 200 others. He is one of two people in history to both be elected into the Professional Speaker Hall of Fame and made a Fellow of the Institute of Management Consultants. He's written over 60 books appearing in 13 languages. His latest, released earlier this year, is *Threescore and More* (Taylor and Francis).

He has coached executives and entrepreneurs in nearly 60 countries. He is interviewed and quoted frequently in the media. *Success* magazine has cited him in an editorial devoted to his work as "a worldwide expert in executive education." The *New York Post* called him "one of the most highly regarded independent consultants in America." His annual Thought Leadership Conference has included guests such as James Carville, Marshall Goldsmith, Dan Pink, and Robert Cialdini. He has been married for 50 years to his high school sweetheart, Maria.

Further Resources

Alan Weiss, PhD
President
Summit Consulting Group, Inc.
Box 1009
East Greenwich, RI 02818
Phone: 401/884-2778 Fax: 401/884-5068
Alan@summitconsulting.com
http://www.summitconsulting.com
http://contrarianconsulting.com

Visit Our Website For:

- Subscription to our free monthly electronic newsletters: *Balancing Act: Blending Life, Work, and Relationships, Monday Morning Memo, Million Dollar Consulting® Mindset, Monday Morning Memo*
- Inclusion on our notification list for new products, workshops, and services
- Access to over 1,000 free indexed articles

Index